Enterprising Slaves & Master Pirates

PETER LANG
New York • Washington, D.C./Baltimore • Bern
Frankfurt am Main • Berlin • Brussels • Vienna • Oxford

Virgil Henry Storr

Enterprising Slaves & Master Pirates

UNDERSTANDING ECONOMIC LIFE IN THE BAHAMAS

PETER LANG
New York • Washington, D.C./Baltimore • Bern
Frankfurt am Main • Berlin • Brussels • Vienna • Oxford

Library of Congress Cataloging-in-Publication Data

Storr, Virgil Henry.
Enterprising slaves and master pirates: understanding economic life
in the Bahamas / Virgil Henry Storr.
p. cm.
Includes bibliographical references (p.) and index.
1. Bahamas—Economic conditions. 2. Entrepreneurship—Bahamas.
3. Slaves—Bahamas. 4. Pirates—Bahamas. 5. Economics—
Sociological aspects. I. Title.
HC152.S76 330.97296—dc22 2003022531
ISBN 0-8204-7075-9

Bibliographic information published by **Die Deutsche Bibliothek**.
Die Deutsche Bibliothek lists this publication in the "Deutsche
Nationalbibliografie"; detailed bibliographic data is available
on the Internet at http://dnb.ddb.de/.

Cover design by Joni Holst

The paper in this book meets the guidelines for permanence and durability
of the Committee on Production Guidelines for Book Longevity
of the Council of Library Resources.

275 Seventh Avenue, 28th Floor, New York, NY 10001
www.peterlangusa.com

Printed in Germany

For Don and Uncle Chuck

Contents

Chapter One
Introduction

Once upon a time was a very old time,
Monkey chew tobacco an' he spit white lime.
Well it wasn't my time and it wasn't your time,
It was old time.[1]

West Indian economic histories are typically agricultural stories. They are usually dramatic tales about the successes and failures of King Sugar and his subjects. They are usually ghastly tales about British absentee owners, brutal slave drivers, brutalized African slaves and indentured Indian laborers. They are typically tales set on a plantation. They are typically plantation narratives. Indeed, West Indian economies have been and (for the most part) continue to be plantation hinterlands. Their economies continue to be dependent on "imported enterprise," the "locus of key [economic] decisions [remains] metropolitan" and the *raison d'être* of economic life is still "to produce a staple required for metropolitan consumption and for entrepot trade to third countries" (Levitt and Best 1993, 408). As such, the economic histories of Jamaica, Trinidad, Barbados, St. Lucia, St. Vincent and Guyana are all very similar. The story of the Bahamas, however, does not read like other West Indian narratives. In fact, the plantation system, which thrived and continues to thrive elsewhere in the region, never really "got off the ground" in the Bahamas.[2]

Why didn't the plantation system succeed in the Bahamas? Primarily, because Bahamian soils are "thin, scattered, and easily exhausted" (Craton and Saunders 1992, 196). As McKinnen wrote, "although nature in all of . . . (the [Bahamian] islands) . . . spontaneously brings forth many vegetables both curious and beautiful, she has hitherto refused to resign herself to continued cultivation" (Albury 1975, 116). Bahamian soils were, thus, never suited for the rigors of sugar production and, although cotton cultivation had been tried in earnest throughout the 1780s, by the end of that decade the industry had collapsed. In fact, "the clearing of the natural cover for making cotton fields, coupled with the occasional heavy rains, speeded erosion and the leaching of what soils there were" (Craton and Saunders 1992, 196). But, if not sugar or cotton or some other commercial crop, then who was the star of economic life in the Bahamas? And, if not the usual tale of the rise and fall of King Sugar (by 1667 sugar was certainly king in the West Indies), what is the Bahamas' story?

The canonical histories would have us believe that the Bahamian story is a simple tale of *economic woe*, of *boom and bust*. Consequently, they merely catalogue the momentary booms that the Bahamas has enjoyed and the protracted busts that always followed.[3] That the enterprises that triggered and sustained the successive booms were very similar to each other, however, is an argument that is often suggested but is seldom explored.[4]

Throughout its history the Bahamas has proven to be a paradise for those who would engage in illegal and extra-legal enterprises. Pirates and privateers based in the Bahamas captured and plundered unsuspecting ships laden with gold and wares, disrupting trade flows between the new world and the old, and escaping with extra-ordinary returns for their efforts. *Wreckers* lured passing ships onto the unforgiving coral reefs that surround the islands of the Bahamas in order to loot and pillage. Blockade runners smuggled guns to the Confederate Army during the American Civil War, rum runners smuggled alcohol into the U.S. during Prohibition and drug dealers have smuggled vast amounts of illegal drugs into America during the latter part of the twentieth century. Although the activities attempted during the successive declines were diverse and often dissimilar, all of the significant economic upswings in the first five centuries of

Bahamian history (1492-1992) have been fueled by "piratical" enterprises (i.e. enterprises that were at best morally and legally dubious).

The canonical histories of the Bahamas have, nonetheless, only hinted at the similarities between all of the Bahamas' successful industries. Likewise, they have only hinted at the link between the peculiar character of Bahamian slavery and the *spirit of enterprise* that so infects Bahamian people.[5] Bahamian slavery was indeed peculiar. Nuclear families were remarkably stable amongst Bahamian slaves and slaves in the Bahamas were much healthier than slaves in Barbados, Trinidad, Jamaica, Haiti or Cuba. Similarly, Bahamian slaves seem to have had more "free" time, enjoyed much more autonomy (they could contract out their own labor) and attained a higher standard of living (if you can call a slave's existence living), than their Caribbean cousins. Consequently, Bahamian slaves, to an even greater degree than slaves elsewhere in the region, metamorphosed into a proto-peasantry (growing their own provisions and marketing surplus produce and dry goods in spite of their chattel status). And, unlike their Caribbean cousins, Bahamian blacks, even when they were slaves, developed and manned a "prosperous" service economy.

The economic story of the Bahamas can, thus, be read as a tale of *enterprising slaves* and *master pirates,* of the indelible mark they have made on economic life in the Bahamas and the significant roles they have played in the Bahamian narrative. This study will attempt to tell and interpret the Bahamas' unusual story. In so doing, it moves us away from cliometrics (a la Fogel and others) and towards a more interpretive approach to the study of economic life, that is, it moves us towards an approach to the study of economic history that emphasizes the importance of entrepreneurs to the economic process, that insists on grounding individuals in their historical and cultural contexts and that takes seriously the economist's role as storyteller.

Being a Teller of Stories

Essentially, economic historians (indeed all economists) are "tellers of stories and makers of poems" (McCloskey 1990b, 61). We are weavers of dramatic, analytical narratives with often complex and surprising plots. (The best I think are *bildungsromans*, coming of age tales that focus on how individual actors in a society learn, change and grow, that focus on how actors respond to changing economic, social and political environments.) Economists are as concerned with genre, with plot and character development, with time and place, with characterization, structure and setting, with imagery and irony, with point of view, with theme, style and symbolism as other authors. McCloskey (ibid., 64) has argued that "plainly and routinely, 90 per cent of what economists do is . . . storytelling. Yet even in the other 10 percent, in the part more obviously dominated by models and metaphors, the economist tells stories." According to McCloskey (ibid.; *emphasis hers*),

> The applied economist can be viewed as a realistic novelist or a realist playwright – a Thomas Hardy or a George Bernard Shaw. The theorist, too, may be viewed as a teller of stories, though a non-realist – whose plots and characters have the same relation to truth as those in *Gulliver's Travels* or *A Midsummer Night's Dream*. Most economics is saturated with narration.

Regardless of whether an economic tale is science fiction (theoretical) or realistic (historical), however, the main character is often the entrepreneur. Indeed, the entrepreneur is the *sine qua non* of the market process. She is the protagonist; the agent of change in the narrative. If she is reasonably alert to profit opportunities and is unimpeded and unimpaired in her efforts to exploit them, that is, if she is (and is allowed to be) reasonably innovative, economic progress is likely to occur. If there are (real or imagined) barriers to entrepreneurship, however, economic progress is likely to be thwarted. The ability of entrepreneurs to act as the driving force of an economy, therefore, has a lot to do with the degree of government intervention into the economic system, the availability of capital and credit, the quantity and quality of available laborers and the attitudes regarding entrepreneurship that pervade their cultures.

Entrepreneurs are cultural creatures. As such, it matters what their culture's models of economic success are, how they are portrayed by their society's culture industry and how they fare in their culture's fables and myths. That is, it matters whether they are celebrated or profaned, whether they are conceived of as heroes or leeches, whether entrepreneurial efforts are thought of as futile or gainful. The best economic narratives recognize this and so are social novels that embed their characters in ongoing social relations. A tale of the last two centuries of economic life in America, for example, would have to at least mention the myth and lure of realizing the American Dream (the notion that hard work equals economic prosperity) if it is to account for that nation's unparalleled prosperity; that myth has, arguably, been as important to America's development as its natural endowments.

Similarly, understanding that the "art of profit-seeking" and the "act of theft" is conflated in the Russian consciousness (practitioners of both are called Mafiosi) is critical to appreciating the perils of post-Soviet transition in Russia. This *miseducation*, the legacy of over half-a-century of Soviet rule, has impeded and impaired entrepreneurial discoveries in Russia and has prevented many Russians from participating fully in the (post-Soviet) economic life of that country. Indeed, a country's "cultural legacy" can have a profound effect on its economic success and economists *qua* storytellers must be aware that a country's models of economic success can color entrepreneurial efforts.

Additionally, economists *qua* storytellers must be aware of *peripety* i.e. that an event, a shock, can dramatically alter the plot. Economists must be aware that a happening or an episode in a country's, in a people's, history can propel them along a trajectory that was quite different than the path they were on previously. Colonialism, for instance, was a plot altering experience. It altered the course of history in India, Africa and the Americas and profoundly affected the lives of those "native" peoples and their descendents. It also "taught" the colonized to doubt the possibility of their attaining entrepreneurial success (at least in the absence of political connections and patronage) and to view government as an engine for economic progress.[6] Colonialism must, therefore, factor prominently in any development narrative. It must be at the fore of any attempt to understand why no dynamic class of entrepreneurs has developed in much of Africa, the Caribbean or Latin America. Ultimately, economists *qua* storytellers are in the business of telling culturally aware, historical narratives. How then can we tell tales that present the diverse and rich historical, geographic, political, economic and social backdrops against which all individual actions are negotiated and interpreted? How do we understand the cultural context ("the web of meanings") in which an individual lives? I propose, concurring with Lavoie and Chamlee-Wright (2001, 22), that we get at culture "by way of intimate, detailed, qualitative research, immersed in the complex context of *one* particular situation," that we get at culture by reading cultural texts.

Gadamer (1986) has written eloquently about how we read/interpret/understand the pictures, paintings, poems, plans, actions, stories, lives and contexts, in short, the "texts" of others. As Gadamer (ibid., 68) writes, interpretation is how we get at meaning ("it is unitary with understanding") and, consequently, involves either "pointing to something" or "pointing out the meaning of something." Rather than "reading in some meaning," however, interpretation is "clearly a revealing of what the thing itself already points to." Interpretation, Gadamer correctly surmises, is only necessary when the text we wish to interpret has a "multiplicity of meaning." As he (ibid.) suggests, "we do not have to interpret or scrutinize an unambiguous statement or order that simply requires obedience. We have only to interpret something when its meaning is not clearly laid down or when it is ambiguous."

Interpreting the meaning of a statement (or action or any other text), however, does not mean divining the author's intention. Indeed, "what the poet [or author or actor] intends is in no way superior to what anyone else intends" (ibid., 72). The text, if you will, has something to say; something not entirely divorced but most definitely distinct from the author's intentions. As Gadamer (1976, 57) asserts, "when [the text] does begin to speak it does not simply speak its word, always the same, in lifeless rigidity, but gives ever new answers to the person who . . . questions it and poses ever new questions to him who answers it. To understand a text is to come to understand oneself in a kind of dialogue." What we draw out of a text, how we understand a text, has everything to do with the questions we ask it (ibid.).[7] This is not to say, however, that a text can say anything. That the meaning of a text is not "always the same, in lifeless rigidity" should not be taken as a retreat into nihilistic relativism. Rather, it is an acknowledgement that all interpretations, all understandings, are partial, that any interpretation obscures some aspects of the text while highlighting others, that the interpreters own prejudices and proclivities shape both what we can see in the text and what we can say about it (Wachterhauser 1999, 94).

Recognizing that it is not just the author's intentions that we are seeking to reveal, that interpretation is instead a dialogue between the interpreter (the human scientist, the economist) and the text (the action), is at the heart of the *compositive method* championed by Menger, Mises and Hayek.[8] Consider, for instance, the Austrian tale about the evolution of money. Imagine, they insist, a context where there is no indirect (money) exchange; all trade is barter. For barter exchange to be successful, however, there must be a double coincidence of wants. An individual who grows corn and hopes to buy bananas, for instance, has to find someone in the market who both has bananas and wants corn in order to complete a successful exchange. Eventually, someone will recognize that they can get more of what they want from their trip to the market (that they can complete more trades) by first trading the goods they produce (corn in my example) for an intermediate, more marketable good (e.g. salt) and then trading that more marketable commodity for the commodity they really desire (bananas in my example). As more and more people in a particular community turn to indirect exchange a smaller and smaller group of commodities emerge as the most marketable.

Ultimately, one commodity (cowry shells in one context, gold in another) emerges as the most marketable and that good is money.

Notice that it is not only the actors' intentions that are highlighted in this story. The traders are not trying to create money but simply to reduce their costs of transacting. The traders do not intend money but we understand their actions as leading to money's creation. Notice also that culture "shows up" at several critical junctures in this narrative. Culture both determines which goods emerge as the most marketable (cowry shells in one context, gold in another) and how quickly a monetary standard becomes established; culture is reasonably thought of as "the cumulative experience of past generations."

Understanding/interpretation should, thus, be seen as a constructive/creative process. It is arrived at through a process of inquiry where questions are asked of the text (the actions of individuals in a barter economy) and answers sought (how individuals come to create money although they do not intend it). As Gadamer (1960, 280) argues, "the meaning of a text surpasses its author not occasionally, but always. Thus understanding is not a reproductive procedure, but rather always also a productive one . . . It suffices to say that one understands *differently when one understands at all.*"

Engaging in this "productive process" is precisely what goes on in critical studies, women's studies, black studies, cultural studies, etc. And, reading *cultural texts* is precisely what anthropologists are doing when they make ethnographic contact. Indeed, ethnography is a hermeneutical project. It is not just an effort to divine what the subjects intend by their actions but an attempt to render clearly what the texts of their lives intimate. Unfortunately, many anthropologists are not clear about just what they are doing when they act as participant-observers and many are unaware of the epistemological limits of their (participant-observer) method. Many believe, for instance, that it is possible to actually "come to interpret the world in the same way" as the people they are studying (Hammersley and Atkinson 1995, 8). As Hammersley and Atkinson (1995, 17) acknowledge, however, "there is no way in which we can escape the social world in order to study it." And, as Hammersley and Atkinson (ibid., 18) concede, "accounts of the world are produced through selective observation and theoretical interpretation of what is seen, through asking particular questions and interpreting what is said in reply, through writing fieldnotes and transcribing audio- and video-recordings, as well as through writing research reports." Again, interpretation is a "productive" process.

An economic analysis that appreciates culture, necessarily engages in this sort of production. That is precisely what I intend to do here. To re-read, to reinterpret, indeed to reconstruct the economic history of the Bahamas as a story of *enterprising slaves* and *master pirates.* To construct what is (I hope) a compelling analytical narrative of economic life in the Bahamas. So, let me tell you a story!

Chapter Summary

Chapter Two, "Context Matters: The Importance of Time and Place in Economic Narratives" attempts to construct a cultural economics consistent with the interpretive social science of Weber, Mises and Hayek. Beginning with a description of the Weber-Austrian approach, the chapter moves very quickly to a discussion of why the study of culture is important to any attempt to understand economic phenomena and how we might bring the study of culture into our understanding of economics. As I conclude, ours is a science of meanings and as such a focus on culture must be at the fore of our analysis.

In *Chapter Three, "Expulsis Piratis: Piracy as a Model and Metaphor for Economic Success,"* I argue that the country's pirate past has affected the way that Bahamian entrepreneurs view business. I, therefore, begin the chapter by describing some of the similarities between the pirate-like industries that have succeeded in the Bahamas. Next, I argue that *piracy* is often celebrated in Bahamian culture. The trickster, for instance, is a popular hero in Bahamian folklore and Bahamian cultural texts often revel in the Bahamas' pirate past. I, then, end the chapter with a description of the *master pirate,* the first of the two ideal types of the Bahamian entrepreneur that I develop in this project. Like Kirzner's entrepreneur her chief characteristic is alertness, but unlike Kirzner's she is not alert to profit opportunities, per se. Rather, she is alert to profiteering opportunities. She views her relationship with her neighbors as a necessarily parasitic one and sees prohibitions by foreign and local governments on their citizens as an opportunity for economic success.

In *Chapter Four, "Sankofa: The Peculiar Nature of Bahamian Slavery,"* I present the second ideal type of the Bahamian entrepreneur, *the enterprising slave.* Unlike the *master pirate,* the *enterprising slave* believes that success is possible through hard work even in the face of extraordinary obstacles. I begin the chapter, however, by discussing slavery in the Caribbean. Throughout the Caribbean, slaves were given the land and the time to grow their own provisions and had the right to consume and market any surpluses that resulted from their efforts. This practice, we shall see, gave voice to the *spirit of enterprise* that so infects African and West Indian peoples. I then draw attention to some of the salient characteristics of slavery in the Bahamas. As stated earlier, Bahamian slavery was a peculiar institution. Slaves in the Bahamas, for instance, were often given the same share as free laborers (white or black) on fishing and wrecking expeditions and were allowed to rent out their labor to the highest bidder so long as they met the cost of their own upkeep and paid their owners a fixed fee. Arguably, the experiences they gained negotiating wages, developing and marketing their skills, in short, the experiences they gained manning and developing a service economy, prepared Bahamians "culturally" to exploit the opportunities (both piratical and legitimate) with which they were presented.

Chapter Five, "Using Metaphors: Explaining Enterprise in the Bahamas," then attempts to put it all together. Beginning with a discussion of how these two competing/complimentary views of entrepreneurship have affected business practices in the Bahamas, I then examine how these orientations to business life, how the presence of both *enterprising slaves* (who work hard in spite of oppressive constraints) and *master pirates* (alert to profiteering opportunities) have affected and been affected by the two dominant export industries in the Bahamas, off-shore banking and tourism. I then conclude this study, in *Chapter 6,* with a review of the main argument presented here: that the story of the Bahamas is meaningfully retold as a tale of *enterprising slaves* and *master pirates.*

Notes

[1] Traditional Bahamian refrain, often recited before recounting a story or telling a folktale in the Bahamas.

[2] As Strachan (1995,190) notes, "plantation economy" is a recent phenomenon in the Bahamas; it "never flourished [there] until *tourism.*" Strachan thinks this is ironic. As he (ibid., 191) suggests, "those who wished to institute the plantation economy [in the Bahamas] were unable to find the right product to use as its foundation or exercised poor judgment in their methods of production. Ultimately, the perceived beauty of the sea, the 'unproductive' landscape, the warm climate, proved to be the long sought-after resources that would bring profit to those with the capital to orchestrate their exploitation, and the hotel would be the institution that would make plantationesque economics work in the Bahamas."

[3] I say merely catalogue here not to downplay the accomplishment. To be sure, in providing us with an organized account of what has happened they have done us an invaluable service. As Thompson (1979, viii) says of his *An Economic History of the Bahamas,* "this book is by no means exhaustive. It will have served its purpose by acting as a catalyst for additional research into and indeed analysis of the various stages of development which our economy has undergone." But, even those histories which intended (in as much as possible) to be exhaustive – for example, Albury (1975) and Craton ([1962] 1986) – do not go far enough in drawing parallels between the successive booms.

[4] See Craton and Saunders (1992), *Islanders in the Stream: A History of the Bahamian People,* for a notable exception.

[5] See Johnson (1996), *The Bahamas from Slavery to Servitude: 1783-1933,* for an important exception.

[6] See Storr (2002) and Butkevich and Storr (2001).

[7] Dewey has also made this point concerning the *primacy of the question.* As Dewey ([1938] 1991, 109) suggests, "inquiry and questioning, up to a certain point, are synonymous terms. We inquire when we question; and we inquire when we seek for whatever will provide an answer to a question asked." Inquiry, thus, necessarily begins with a question, or rather, inquiry necessarily begins in a questionable situation.

[8] As Schutz (1932, 113) suggests, although we should begin by trying to understand the 'meaning an action has for an actor,' we should not stop there, but should also consider the broader significance of that action. As Boettke (1995b, 63) describes, for Schutz, "the task, therefore, for the political economist is, first, render intelligible economic phenomena in terms of the purposes and plans of social actors involved and, second, trace out the unintended consequences, both desirable and undesirable, of those actions. In the tracing of unintended consequences the social theorist must assess the *significance* of events."

Chapter Two

Context Matters: The Importance of Time and Place in Economic Narratives

Introduction

How do we come to understand the thoughts, words and deeds of others? Why, for instance, do we think of Romeo and Juliet as "star-crossed lovers"? Why are they seen as tragic figures and not, say, as foolish romantics? Why, for instance, aren't we disturbed by Hamlet's madness or surprised by Macbeth's fear of Macduff? Why do we believe Richard when he offers his kingdom for a horse? The answers to all of these queries, me thinks, is that we can understand others (be they characters in a Shakespearian play, historical figures or our contemporaries) because we can appreciate their historical and cultural circumstances. That is, we can understand the actions of others (we can understand their life stories) because we can appreciate their prejudices and constraints; we can appreciate the effect that the past (i.e. prior events in the plot) might have had on their proclivities and opportunity sets; we can appreciate the time and place in which they live and act.

Indeed, context matters. Knowing their circumstances, for instance, it would be difficult to view Romeo and Juliet as anything but star-crossed. An "ancient grudge" divides their "two households, [though] both [are] alike in dignity" and so the consequences of their falling in love with each other were bound to be dire. That they had to marry in secret, that Romeo would kill Tybalt, Juliet's cousin, less than a day after that secret marriage, that Juliet would rather fake her death than tell her parents of her marriage all makes sense given the "ancient grudge" that separated the families of Romeo and Juliet. Their double-suicide saddens but does not "surprise" us. Similarly, we understand the stories of Richard III, Macbeth and Hamlet because we understand the time and place in which they are set; we understand the characters' historical and cultural contexts.

Understanding the actions of others requires the same sort of appreciation for time and place, for setting, for context, that understanding a Shakespearean plot requires. A science, like economics, predicated on understanding the meanings that individuals associate with their actions and primarily concerned with telling stories must, therefore, be preoccupied with context. Individuals are not atomistic creatures but are, instead, social characters. They "do not behave or decide to behave as atoms outside a social context" (Granovetter 1985, 487). Rather, they are members of families, of clubs, of bowling leagues, of churches and of communities; they are employers or employees; they are citizens of countries with particular ethnicities. They are not, however, social automata. Individuals do not "adhere slavishly to a script written for them by the particular intersection of social categories that they happen to occupy" (ibid., 487). They do not "follow customs, habits or norms automatically and unconditionally" (ibid., 483). Romeo, for instance, still falls in love with Juliet although he is a Montague and she is a Capulet.

Unfortunately, many in the human sciences have fallen prey to the pitfalls of positing either an *over-* or *under-socialized* view of the individual and so have failed to recognize that an individual's behavior may be "*affected* by, *influenced* by, even *directed* by social structures and relations but [is] not determined by them" (Boettke and Storr 2002; *italics theirs*). Max Weber and the Austrian School (headed by Mises and Hayek), however, have proposed an *interpretive social science,* a *social economics,* that avoids both the *over-* or *under-*

socialized misconceptions of the individual (ibid.). This interpretive science, I contend, is the appropriate vehicle for the study of economic culture (particularly, and we shall see why later, the culture of entrepreneurship) and, so, in this chapter, I intend to push at the boundaries of Weber and the Austrians' *social economics* to see if it is up to this task.

The Weber-Austrian Approach: The Case for the Tri-Embedded Actor

For Weber, "social economics deals with those phenomena that are scarce, that are necessary to satisfy ideal and material interests, and that can only be provided through planning, struggle, and in cooperation with other people" (Swedberg 1998, 192). As such, "it draws on elements from both historical and theoretical economics" (ibid.). "The range of social-economics," according to Weber, "is [thus] almost overwhelming" (Weber [1949] 1997, 66) covering the study of (a) *economic,* (b) *economically relevant* and (c) *economically conditioned* phenomena and institutions.

The first of these categories refer to "events and constellations of norms, institutions, etc., the economic aspect of which constitutes their primary cultural significance for us" (Weber [1949] 1997, 64). Customs like satisfying open accounts within thirty days, institutions like money and credit and organizations like banks and the stock exchange, that is, phenomena which interest us primarily because of their economic significance, thus, fall within this category. As we can see, unlike mainstream economics, Weber's interpretive science was at its core an institutional economics. Weber knew full well that *institutions matter* and believed that *looking at institutions is critical* even when considering purely economic phenomena. As such, the institution-less, a-contextual *homoeconomicus* never played a role in Weber's *social economics.* That Weber extended the range of his science beyond the study of economic phenomena in the strictest sense, however, only served to deepen the chasm between the economic agent of Weber's thought and his cousin in the mainstream.

Weber was not only concerned with pure economic phenomena but also with "all the activities and situations constituting an historically given culture [that] affect the formation of the material wants, the mode of their satisfaction, the integration of interest-groups and the types of power which they exercise" (Weber [1949] 1997, 66). Phenomena like religious sentiments, political beliefs and aesthetic considerations, as Weber points out, do not primarily interest us because of their "economic significance" but they are *economically relevant*; they have "consequences which are of interest from the economic point of view" (Weber [1949] 1997, 64). These phenomena, though not economic in the strict sense, affect the nature of economic life and/or the course of economic development.

Although much of Weber's work in applied *Sozialökonomik* focused on *economically relevant phenomena,* he was aware that the relationship between economic and other social phenomena is not so one-sided and that another category of economic phenomena exists. The third category of his social economics, thus, concerns *economically conditioned phenomena,* that is, "non-economic phenomena that are directly influenced by economic phenomena" (Swedberg 1998, 193). Recognizing that material considerations affect everything from the composition of the law to the structure of the family to the aesthetic values that exist in a given context, I should note, is not a unique insight of Weber. Marx, you may remember, argued that the superstructure (i.e. the organization of the state and the socio-political mores that prevail in a society) has its foundation in the base (i.e. the organization of the means of production in that society). As such, "any particular set of economic relations determines the existence of specific forms of state and social consciousness" (Larrain 1983, 45). While not embracing the totality of Marx's historical materialist claims, Weber's schema does intend to capture (albeit in a weaker form) this aspect of Marx's thought. Public choice and new institutionalist arguments that economic considerations and incentives impact constitutional, legislative and regulatory decision making would also be included in this category of Weber's schema.

In an article entitled *Post Classical Political Economy: Polity, Society and Economy in Weber, Mises and Hayek* (2002), Boettke and Storr tease out the intellectual links between Weber's *Sozialökonomik* and the Austrian school of economics (lead by Mises and Hayek). As Boettke and Storr (2002, 173) assert, "Weber and the Austrians have a deep and symbiotic relationship; they share many of the same intellectual forebears and a commitment to the same methodological approach." Weber, Mises and Hayek were all a part of the same research program.[1]

Boettke and Storr (2002, 168) enlist the imagery of "three circles of potentially different sizes, representing the society, the polity and the economy respectively" in order to describe the unique character of the Weber-Austrian approach. If we were to arrange these circles into a configuration that would reflect Marx's materialist arguments, Boettke and Storr (ibid.) assert, we would have to place the circles representing the society and the polity within the economy circle. Although Marx is correct in asserting that economic factors affect the society and the polity, as Boettke and Storr (ibid.) argue, "there is nothing logically inconsistent with imagining an [alternate] configuration." The economy, for instance, could be placed within the polity and the society; economic activity could be viewed as always occurring in a context of "concrete ongoing social relations." According to Boettke and Storr (ibid.), this configuration, with the circle representing the economy located within the polity and society circles, is precisely the configuration that Granovetter had in mind when he developed his embeddedness arguments.[2] In an article that Swedberg (1991, 268) described as a key article in the "new sociology of economic life," Granovetter, like Weber and the Austrians, calls attention to the social context in which individuals live and act. Unlike Weber and the Austrians, however, Granovetter does not seem to recognize that some social relations may be economically conditioned.

Indeed, the essential idea of the Weber-Austrian approach is that the individual is embedded in the polity, the economy and the society. Rather than privileging Marx's or Granovetter's configuration, Weber and the Austrians "suggests a third way of conceiving the relationship between the society, the economy and the polity" (Boettke and Storr 2002). As Boettke and Storr (ibid., emphasis added) argue,

> Whereas the embeddedness argument suggests that we place the economy within the society and Marx's materialist arguments suggest the opposite, Weber's insistence that we consider both economically relevant and economically conditioned phenomena suggests that we view the economy, the society and the polity as three overlapping circles. The society, the polity and the economy are elevated, if you will, to the same level of prominence and *dual, and treble notions of embeddedness are conceived of and utilized.*

Stated another way, Weber and the Austrians, by focusing on *economically relevant* and *economically conditioned phenomena,* have moved beyond both the single embeddedness of Granovetter and the historical materialism of Marx, and have instead proposed a *treble embedded* individual. As Weber asserts, "the boundary lines of 'economic' phenomena are vague and not easily defined" (Weber [1949] 1997, 65) and, as a result, discussing economic activity without acknowledging its political and economic aspects, without discussing the "social mores and political and legal institutions" which affect and influence it, becomes nearly impossible in his schema. Similarly, discussing social or political activity becomes nearly impossible without discussing their economic aspects.

According to Boettke and Storr, Weber and the Austrians were able to move beyond the problems of Marxian materialism and the incompleteness of Gronovetter's "single" embeddedness arguments by embracing *verstehen*. Weber and the Austrians are chiefly concerned with the meanings that individuals attach to their actions and to their circumstances, that is, the meanings they attach to the geographic, economic, social and historical places where they act and to the times in which they live. "Social phenomena, social structures, social relationships and social actions are unintelligible [for Weber and the Austrians] without considering how actors subjectively perceive them" (ibid.).

Their commitment to *verstehen* thus leads them to situate the actor within a *context of ongoing social meanings;* to conceive of her as both an influencer of the *context of meanings* in which she is located and as being influenced by that context (ibid.). As Boettke and Storr (ibid.) asserted, the Weber-Austrian approach "neither proceeds with disembodied actors, unaffected by the social institutions within which their actions are embedded, nor with social structures and relations dissociated from the web of meanings that give them life." What distinguishes economic phenomena from social and political phenomena, in Weber and Mises and Hayek, is, therefore, "only the meaning[s] that actors attach to them and the context within which actions are attributed meaning[s]" (ibid.). Boettke and Storr position the Weber-Austrian approach as an *economics of meaning*. Where these meanings come from and how some phenomena come to be viewed as political and others as economic or social are questions that Boettke and Storr leave unresolved. In that article our task was principally to show the parallels in Weber, Mises and Hayek and to argue that they were able to articulate a rich conception of embeddedness because of their commitment to *verstehen*. Although my co-author and I identified a *treble embeddedness* argument in Weber, Mises and Hayek, we stopped short of articulating the full implications of their *verstehen* commitment: a commitment to meaning *ipso facto* moves the study of culture to the fore of the analysis. In fact, we may have confused/conflated society with culture in that project.[3]

Culture: Meaning Underneath the Social, the Economic and the Political

Society, as such, is not the same thing as culture. Culture is, in fact, a much broader concept. It is the background against which all (political, social and economic) activity takes place. It is, as Lavoie and Chamlee-Wright (2001, 14) assert, "an *aspect* of virtually any casual factor one might identify, not a separate causal factor of its own. It is the background that provides the linguistic framework with which we understand the world around us." It is, therefore, my conjecture that a focus on the meanings that actors associate with their actions and contexts, a focus required by a commitment to the method of *verstehen*, means that we must focus on culture. This elevation of culture to the fore of our economic, political and social analyses will, I contend, improve our understanding of, amongst other things, the nature of entrepreneurship (Lavoie 1991, 1994), the meaning of prices (Ebeling 1990), the problems of transition (Boettke 2001) and development (Boettke 2001; Butkevich and Storr 2001; Chamlee-Wright 1997, 2000a, 2000b; Storr 2002) and the institutional organization of the economy (Bird-David 1990, 1992; Geertz 1963; Gudemann 1986).

Bird-David (1990, 1992a, 1992b), for instance, in articulating an interpretive approach to economic anthropology, has argued that cultures organize their (economic) activities and relationships on the basis of what she calls "primary metaphors." These metaphors, also called local economic models (see Gudemann 1986), "not only offer [a] means of 'seeing' the world but also govern everyday functioning [of the individuals who hold them] down to the most mundane details" (Bird-David 1990, 190). As such, they offer us a way of understanding economic life in contexts that are even *radically dissimilar* to the environments with which we are familiar. Amongst the Nayaka, a society of gatherer-hunters in Southern India, for instance, the forest is viewed as a parent; that is, the "forest as a parent" is the primary metaphor.[4] As Bird-David (1990, 190) explains, the Nayaka "look on the forest as they do on a mother or a father. For them, it is not something 'out there' that responds mechanically or passively but like a parent; it provides food unconditionally to its children."[5]

A number of Nayaka practices begin to make sense when we recognize that they believe that the *forest is as a parent*. For instance, their views on land ownership, their practice of distributing the spoils of the hunt based on need instead of concerning themselves with who actually killed or captured the animals, and perhaps even the reason why they do not cultivate the land like many of the communities that live near them (the neighboring Bette and the Mullu Kurumbas, for example, are both agrarian communities), can be explained by reference to the primary metaphor that prevails in that context. As might be expected between siblings (i.e. children of the father forest), the "Nayaka give to each other, request from each other, expect to get what they ask for, and feel obliged to give what they are asked for. They do not give resources to each other in a calculated, foresighted fashion, with a view to receiving something in return, nor do they make claims for debts" (Bird-David 1990, 191).

Similarly, the primary metaphor of the "forest as parent" can be used to explain the Nayaka view of land ownership. The Nayaka are quite familiar with notions of several ownership. To be sure, the obligation to share which dominates that context suggests an acceptance that objects can be legitimately owned or at least possessed. Although they seem to accept that objects can be owned, however, they do not believe that land can be owned; they believe in private property but not in real estate. Remember, the Nayaka view each other as siblings, children of the forest. They "believe that the forest as parent gives wild resources to all Nayaka, that is, that all Nayaka are born with rights of direct personal access to land and unearned resources" (Bird-David 1990, 192).

Bird-David (1992a) has found similar patterns of economic organization and similar belief systems operating amongst the Batek of Malaysia and the Mbuti of Zaire. Like the Nayaka, the Batek and the Mbuti are hunter-gather societies with immediate-return systems. While the primary metaphor at work amongst the Nayaka was the *forest as parent*, the primary metaphor amongst the Batek and the Mbuti is one of *sharing*. "Through their close interaction with the environment they have come to perceive it, and act with it," according to Bird-David (1992a, 31), "as with a friend, a relative, a parent who shares resources with them." These hunter-gatherers, thus, behave as if resources are not scarce but in abundance; "they enjoy and exhaust what they have obtained, however much it is, and persist in their demands for shares, irrespective of what they already have" (ibid.)

That cultural characteristics and metaphors can and do influence the pattern of economic organization across contexts has also been suggested by Lipset's (1990) comparison of values and institutions in the United States and Canada. Canadian businessmen, Lipset (1990, 120) points out, are often described as being "less aggressive, less innovative, [and] less risk-taking than their American counterparts." These differences in entrepreneurial cultures seem to have stemmed from more general differences in the national identities of these two neighbors. Americans are harder working and more concerned with material success while Canadians are more cautious and more concerned with their quality of life or so the stereotypes go. Public opinion polls (cited by Lipset), however, seem to confirm these stereotypes. In Gallup and market research polls taken in the late 70s and early 80s, Canadians appeared to be more reluctant to try new products and less likely to invest in research and development than their American cousins. Similarly, Canadians tended to pursue more conservative investment strategies than American investors.

Not surprisingly then, as a result of these cultural differences, that is, these differences in national cultural identities, the Canadian economy has come to be organized quite differently from the U.S. economy. "The Canadian economy," according to Lipset (1990, 130), is "organized more like the economies of Europe than that of the United States." There is "a much greater concentration of ownership and control among Canadian corporations than American firms" (Lipset 1990, 129). Business networks in Canada are more closely tied (are more dense) than they are in the United States and Canadian firms have a greater proportion of directors in common than firms south of the border.[6] The anti-elitist, anti-big-business sentiments that color business practices in the United States and have been institutionalized into that nation's regulatory environment are not as prevalent in the Canadian context. And, in Canada even the weak anti-trust legislation that exists is rarely enforced. Lipset's study thus suggests that differences in cultural identities, even the necessarily subtle differences that exist between peoples living in close proximity to one another, can have a dramatic effect on the way economies come to be organized and regulated and on the business practices that evolve across contexts.

Similarly, Geertz's (1963) investigation of social development and economic change in Modjokuto and Tabanan, two towns in Indonesia, bears out the contention defended again here (and suggested also by Bird-David's and Lipset's work) that context matters.[7] Geertz's ground-breaking study, *Peddlers and Princes* (1963), compared economic life in Modjokuto, in eastern central Java, and Tabanan, in southwest Bali. Modjokuto is a small Javanese sea port where "the market forms the hub of a far-flung and intensely active trade network through which a fabulous variety of goods flow and from which probably a majority of the town population in one way or another draws its living" (Geertz 1963, 8). In Indonesia, generally, and Java, in particular, Modjokuto was unique in this respect. The "trader class" was more numerous in Modjokuto than it was in other Javanese towns of comparable size and the "civil service corps" much smaller. What accounts for these differences? Why has Modjokuto evolved as a town of peddlers when other Javanese towns have not?

According to Geertz, most Javanese towns of Modjokuto's size were regency capitals while Modjokuto was just a district capital. The cadre of public servants, of political and cultural elite, that were attracted to and that came to dominate the social landscape elsewhere in Java were, therefore, not as numerous in Modjokuto. This meant that "the impact upon the town as a whole of the etiquette and the art-centered, heavily Hinduized, court-oriented style of life affected by these aristocrats turned bureaucrats was rather less intense than elsewhere and the domination of their somewhat over-civilized 'high society' less stupefying" (Geertz 1963, 12). In Modjokuto, peddlers, stunted in other Javanese towns, thrived in a cultural landscape more conducive (or rather less hostile) to trade and barter.

The relative absence of an aristocracy, however, was not the only reason that there was a thriving bazaar in Modjokuto. In the late 19th and the early 20th centuries Modjokuto had a booming economy. The textile, tobacco, sugar and rice industries were all expanding rapidly and by 1930 "the urbanization of Modjokuto had been greatly advanced, and the town had become a thriving center of trade" (Geertz 1963, 10). But in the 1930s the plantation economy collapsed and a large number of peasants who hitherto worked as seasonal laborers on the plantations "flooded" the market as "small-scale" traders. Successive declines in the economy led, according to Geertz (1963, 11), to "an intensification rather than a slowing down of economic activity" and continued "the over-all trend toward the conversion of the bulk of the Modjokuto's citizens into small-scale businessmen."[8]

The bustling Modjokuto stands in sharp contrast to Tabanan, a Balinese court town, where it was not "the bazaar but the palace which has stamped its character upon the town, not the Islamized trader but the Hinduized aristocrat who has been its distinctive figure" (Geertz 1963, 18). The population in Tabanan is less dense than it is in Modjokuto (i.e. Tabanan is less urbanized) and its citizens are much less market-oriented. Tabanan is a largely agrarian society where most peasants are able to support themselves through their subsistence activities. Capital-intensive agricultural activities, agricultural wage labor, the renting of rice fields for money and the buying/selling of foodstuffs on the open market, all quite common in Modjokuto, are relatively rare in Tabanan.

Geertz suggests several reasons why Tabanan has had a different development path than Modjokuto. One reason is that the nobility have always been and, indeed, continue to be central to life in Tabanan. Another is that village life in Tabanan is organized into what "is perhaps best seen as a set of the overlapping and intersecting corporate associations the Balinese call *seka*" (Geertz 1963, 84). These *seka* or social groups are each organized to serve some particular political, economic or social function and the Balinese, each of whom belong to between three to a dozen *seka*, are quite loyal to these groups. Consequently, economic activities in Tabanan tend to be strongly collective; cooperatives and even partnerships, quite rare in other parts of Indonesia, are quite common there.

Like Bird-David and Lipset's studies, Geertz's investigation suggests that there is a certain path dependence to economic development. That business practices and entrepreneurial attitudes may differ widely across contexts. And, that the pattern of economic organization that emerges in a particular context is shaped by that community's particular economic history and culture. The disparate histories/cultures of Modjokuto and Tabanan, for instance, have led to economic life being dominated by peddlers in one community and princes in the other.

These moves to offer cultural explanations of social economic phenomena are quite compatible with the *interpretive social science*, the *social economics*, proposed by Weber and developed by Austrian scholars. As argued before, Weber and the Austrians, at least implicitly appreciate the importance of culture. And, insist on recognizing, as Mises does that,

> Inheritance and environment direct a man's actions. They suggest to him both the ends and the means. He lives not simply as man in *abstracto*; he lives as a son of his family, his people, and his age; as a citizen of his country; as a member of a definite social group; as a practitioner of a certain vocation; as a follower of definite religious, metaphysical, philosophical, and political ideas; as a partisan in many feuds and controversies. He does not himself create his ideas and standards of value; he borrows them from other people. His ideology is what his environment enjoins upon him.
>
> (Mises 1949, 46)

Although Mises does not mention the word "culture", it is clear that "inheritance" and "environment", as Mises employs them, and "culture", as I mean it here, are synonymous. As North (1994, 364) argues, culture embodies "the cumulative experience of past generations."[9] Man, for Mises, is, therefore, a *cultural creature*; he does not live in *abstracto*. Indeed, culture directs (but does not determine) his actions and acts as the prism through which he views his problem situation; it "suggests to him both means and ends."

Acknowledging that culture plays a critical role in directing a man's actions, however, does not (by itself) give us any insight into how we might construct a *cultural economics*. Nor, does it suggest how we should incorporate cultural considerations into our analysis or which parts of our science can benefit most from a dose of cultural awareness. There seems to be at least an implicit agreement amongst the proponents of a more culturally attuned economics, however, that the study of entrepreneurship is the area of our science that can benefit most (or most readily) by an engagement with culture. Remember, Geertz's *Peddlers and Princes* (1963) was primarily a study of the way entrepreneurship differed across contexts. Similarly, Berger's *The Cultures of Entrepreneurship* (1991), sponsored by The Institute for the Study of Economic Culture, made a significant contribution to both the study of entrepreneurship and the development of a culturally attuned economics (see particularly Lavoie's and Berger's contribution to that volume). Even in Harrison's two volumes, *Who Prospers* (1992) and *Underdevelopment is a State of Mind* (1985), where he tends to scapegoat rather than incorporate culture, the focus is primarily on how culture impedes or impairs entrepreneurs.

Entrepreneurs in Context: Creating a Cultural Economics

The entrepreneur is at the heart of market processes, at the heart of economic development and, increasingly, at the heart of development theory. Our recognition of these "facts" owes much to Israel Kirzner. Kirzner, building on Mises' contention that, "entrepreneurial perception lies outside of the mechanical perception of choice as optimal resource allocation" (Chamlee-Wright 1997, 44), that is, outside of the rational choice framework employed by neo-classical economists, constructs a theory of entrepreneurship that emphasizes the creative and novel character of entrepreneurial efforts. Admittedly, if human beings lived in a world where actors had perfect knowledge, that is, where all possible means were already identified and all possible ends were already conceived, then Kirzner's emphasis on the extra-optimizing efforts by economic agents would be unnecessary.[10]

But human beings live in a world of radical uncertainty and fundamental ignorance (Mises [1949] 1963; Hayek 1948, 1955; Kirzner

1973, [1979] 1983). Knowledge is not perfect nor is perfectible. As such, there are always means that have not hitherto been identified and ends that have not hitherto been conceived. For instance, buyers in a given locality are often unaware that a good that they desire is available in a neighboring area. Similarly, sellers are often unable to locate their perspective buyers. It is in these "spheres of ignorance" that Kirzner's entrepreneur operates and is effective.[11]

So long as there is ignorance, Kirzner argues, there will be arbitrage opportunities and individuals who are *alert* to them. Stated another way, so long as there are opportunities to buy low in one market and sell high in another, there will be actors who will recognize that opportunity. For Kirzner, an unfocused but nonetheless purposeful, "generalized intentness upon noticing the useful opportunities that may be present within one's field of vision" (Kirzner 1994, 107), that is, an alertness to unexploited opportunities for profit, is, therefore, his entrepreneur's chief characteristic. Although this way of conceiving entrepreneurial activity, as the discovery of new ends and means, and the designation of alertness as the essential trait of entrepreneurs, teaches us quite a bit about the essence of entrepreneurship, it is not without its problems and, as such, it is not without its critics. Don Lavoie, for instance, while maintaining that Kirzner's work is "the best in economics on the subject," has produced several forceful critiques of Kirzner's theory of entrepreneurship (see particularly Lavoie 1991, 1994 and Lavoie and Chamlee-Wright 2000).

For Lavoie (1994, 58), the principal weakness of Kirzner's theory is that it "has not gotten very far in elucidating the cultural dimension" of entrepreneurship. The Kirznerian entrepreneur is ultimately acultural. It is not so much that Kirzner contends that culture does not matter but rather that he (at least in writing) has refused to acknowledge that it does. And, so has not grappled with the consequences of imbuing his entrepreneur with culture. Lavoie offers several reasons why Kirzner has been unable to concede (or possibly recognize) that "entrepreneurship necessarily takes place within culture, [that] it is utterly shaped by culture and [that] it fundamentally consists in interpreting and influencing culture" (Lavoie 1991, 36).

One reason for this inadequacy, according to Lavoie, is that Kirzner trivializes the role of interpretation in the discovery process. Remember, for Kirzner (1979, 148), *entrepreneurial alertness* "consists in the ability to notice without search [,] opportunities that have been hitherto overlooked." Discovering profit opportunities, Kirzner suggests, is like serendipitously finding money on a beach. Indeed, for Kirzner, alertness is a flash of "superior foresight," a discovery of "what is around the corner before others do" (ibid., 8). But, as Lavoie (1991, 44) points out, "most acts of entrepreneurship are not like an isolated individual finding things on beaches; they require efforts of the creative imagination, skillful judgments of future cost and revenue possibilities, and an ability to read the significance of complex social situations."[12]

The entrepreneur does not merely "notice" profits and being alert is not simply "a matter of opening one's eyes to see what is right there under one's nose" (Lavoie 1991, 44). It is not simply a matter of seeing "unambiguous" things that out there just waiting to be grasped. As Lavoie (ibid.) argues, "if entrepreneurship is like vision . . . it is like human vision, which does not see merely patches of color but meaningful things." Ours is a world of plants, and animals, and furniture, and buildings, and automobiles and not simply a world of greens, and grays, and blacks. To be sure, when looking out of our windows we do "see" that there is a red object next to a brown object both sitting below a canopy of blue specked with white; patches of color are not beyond our detection. But, we are also able to recognize those patches as a car, a townhouse and a cloudy sky (with their attending meanings) and to differentiate one from the other.[13] Entrepreneurship, "like visual perception . . . involves seeing an object *as* a certain sort of thing" (Lavoie 1991, 44).

And, as suggested earlier, an entrepreneur interprets what he sees from a particular cultural perceptive. The entrepreneur has a particular "point of view" and the seeing of profit opportunities is not a matter of "objective observation" (as Kirzner implies) but is rather "a discerning of the intersubjective meaning of a qualitative situation", it is, as Lavoie (1991, 36) contends, "a matter of cultural interpretation." Entrepreneurs "read" profit opportunities and this reading takes place within culture. Stated another way, "entrepreneurship is not so much the achievement of an isolated maverick who finds objective profits others overlooked as it is of the culturally embedded participant who picks up the gist of the conversation" (ibid.).

While I agree with Lavoie's contention that recognizing the cultural dimension of entrepreneurship is critical to our being able to understand entrepreneurship and with his contention that this dimension is largely absent in Kirzner's work, I disagree with his assertion that in the end Kirzner's theory "leaves no room for culture" (Lavoie 1994, 58). Kirzner has not, so to speak, closed the door to culture. In fact, many of his statements argue for just the opposite. Kirzner, for instance, was aware that different contexts produced (qualitatively) different kinds of entrepreneurs. He knew full well that there is a difference between an entrepreneur operating in the market and a bureaucrat (see Kirzner 1979, 11).[14] That the entrepreneur living in Soviet Russia behaved differently, faced different incentives, than the entrepreneur living in America was not lost on Kirzner (see, for instance, Kirzner 1979, 11-12). Although Kirzner (1979, 8) was to confess that he did not "clearly understand how entrepreneurs get their flashes of superior insight" he was aware that context mattered. Indeed, if Kirzner's theory of entrepreneurship was not amenable to discussions of culture then Lavoie would have had to discard it. Rather than abandoning Kirzner's work, however, Lavoie (1991, 1994 and with Chamlee-Wright 2000), has proposed several correctives (one more fruitful than the other).

The Limits of Comparative Cultural Advantage and Considering Culture as Capital

One way of constructing a cultural economics might be to extend standard economic concepts so that they address cultural matters.

Lavoie and Chamlee-Wright (2000), for instance, have proposed that we treat aspects as culture in the same way that we do natural resources and that we employ terms like *cultural capital* and *comparative cultural advantage* when considering how culture affects economic behavior. According to Lavoie and Chamlee-Wright (2000, 64),

> Each society has within its grasp a unique repertoire of "cultural resources." Nature endows some societies with rich oil deposits and others with fertile soil. Similar to these natural resources, culture provides some societies with a kinship network conducive to building complex credit markets and other societies with a strong work ethic. Just as markets will develop differently according to their specific natural resources, they will also develop differently according to their cultural resources.

Stated another way, each society has a distinct set of cultural assets (and liabilities) available to its entrepreneurs.

Throsby (2001, 44) has pursued a similar line of inquiry, suggesting that the concept of cultural capital represents cultural phenomena in a way that "captures their essential characteristics in a manner comprehensible within both an economic and a broadly cultural discourse." Cultural capital can thus be seen as bridging the gap between economics on one side and cultural studies and anthropology on the other. And, by treating cultural phenomena (beliefs, customs, practices, languages, values, etc.) as "intangible assets in the possession of the group to which they refer" we can, according to Throsby (ibid., 45) understand the "economic value" of cultural resources.

Of course, we can point out several parallels between cultural capital (as defined by Throsby) and natural capital (as employed by ecological/environmental economists). Nature, goes the argument, has given us an endowment of arable land, and deposits of oil and minerals, and agreeable climates, and, similarly, we've been endowed by our ancestors with certain cultural resources (a strong work ethic in one context, a wide radius of trust in another). There is also an analogy that can be drawn between "the function of natural ecosystems in supporting and maintaining the 'natural balance' and the function of what might be referred to as 'cultural ecosystems' in supporting and maintaining the cultural life and vitality of human civilization" (Throsby 2001, 51).

Rather than making me more comfortable with the concept of cultural capital, however, these similarities have made me more uneasy. In fact, it's the parallels that can be drawn between natural and cultural phenomena that expose the problems inherent in that whole approach. To be sure, there is something about a "cultural ecosystem" that makes it possible for us to think of it in the same way that we might think of a computer, or an automobile, or a machine; (if functioning) it can improve our productivity. But, there is so much that distinguishes cultural phenomena from capital assets. Cultural phenomena are certainly less tradable than traditional capital assets and probably cannot be traded at all (although it is possible to buy/sell cultural artifacts and symbols it is quite another thing to purchase cultural sensibilities and values). Similarly, even though one might contend that cultural assets, like traditional capital assets, have varying degrees of specificity (language, for instance, can support much more activities than, say, an affinity for the color red), it would be extremely difficult and likely impossible to replace a society's current stock of 'cultural capital' for a more appropriate/desirable stock.[15] And, perhaps the most telling, cultural capital does not involve a deliberate sacrifice of present income for future benefits.[16]

Gadamer's ([1966] 1976) discussion of language also proves relevant here. As Gadamer ([1966] 1976, 62) asserts, "language is by no means simply an instrument, a tool. For it is in the nature of the tool that we master its use, which is to say we take it in hand and lay it aside when it has done its service." But, as Gadamer contends, something else is going on when we pluck a set of words from our vocabulary, use them to express this or that thought, and let them return, if you will, to our store of possible words and expressions. Indeed, as Gadamer (ibid.) points out,

> Such an analogy is false because we never find ourselves as consciousness over against the world and, as it were, grasp after a tool of understanding in a wordless condition. Rather, in all our knowledge of ourselves and in all

knowledge of the world, we are always already encompassed by the language that is our own.

The same can be said of culture. We are never able to simply take it off, to set it aside, to be completely free from its affect and influence. I am not suggesting here that we are slaves to our cultural heritages, but as stated before we do not live in *abstracto.* Viewing culture as merely a resource or a tool is, therefore, deeply unsatisfactory.

To my mind, *culture is much more like a constitution than it is like capital.* Remember, constitutions define the formal rules which govern a society. As Hayek (1960, 178) describes, a constitution assigns "specific powers to different authorities," while limiting "their powers not only in regard to the subjects or the aims to be pursued but also with regard to the methods to be employed." A constitution, thus, defines the rules of the games (for the referees and the players, the authorities and individual citizens) and, consequently, both imposes constraints and defines and delimits the set of opportunities that an individual can legitimately exploit. It, therefore, directs an individual away from certain types of activities and towards others; with constitutional rules serving as points of orientation.[17] Culture operates in the same way. Even Throsby (2001, 9) recognizes that "economic agents live, breathe and make decisions within a cultural environment" and that "this environment has some influence on shaping their preferences and regulating their behavior." As such, one wonders if cultural capital is in fact capital at all and whether the concept of cultural comparative advantage can be meaningfully pursued once we recognize that culture cannot satisfactorily be thought of as a resource.

With Ricardo's careful articulation of the law of comparative advantage, we realized that what was important when considering the benefits of trade were not absolute advantages but relative ones. If a Director of Information Technology, for instance, is better at both project management and software development than a particular programmer working for him, it is not necessarily true that he should fire that programmer and perform both functions. Even with the difference in skill levels, the department is probably better off if the manager manages and the programmer programs; they should both specialize in their relative strengths. There are gains to be had from specialization.

For Lavoie and Chamlee-Wright (2001, 65), "the economists' understanding of comparative advantage is a marvelously general notion, as applicable to cultural as it is to material resources." At issue, however, is not

> 'inter-country' comparison, but 'within-country' comparison. It is not whether some kind of aggregated conglomerate of the whole country's values is better than that of another country, but whether the relative cultural strength within a country is, say, its work ethic or its propensity to save; its trust networks or its attitude toward creativity. (ibid.)

Entrepreneurs should, therefore, "work on identifying which elements of their culture are the most promising for them to cultivate in order to achieve what they would consider to be prosperity" (ibid.).

Although on the surface Lavoie and Chamlee-Wright's discussion of *comparative cultural advantages* seems compelling, ultimately notions of comparative cultural advantage (and cultural capital) miss the point. Rather than revealing, as Lavoie and Chamlee-Wright (2000, 66) suggest, "the specific details of any particular culture's comparative advantage," studies of culture offer (and are best situated to offer) us insight into how institutions (necessary for development) might be adapted to fit particular cultural milieus and how different "patterns of entrepreneurship" have been impacted by culture. Cultures simply can not be readily catalogued in terms of their absolute or relative *strengths* and *weaknesses*. Remember, we can not satisfactorily talk in terms of cultural resources.

The problem with the concept of cultural comparative advantage is not that its "wrong" but that it is misleading and terribly inadequate. Lavoie and Chamlee-Wright want to take a concept that has its place within discussions of international trade and use it to make the point that no culture is growth resistant and that all cultures can find ways (possibly quite distinct ways) to grow. While agreeing completely with that sentiment, I have to object strenuously to the path that they have traveled to get us there. It simply does not deal with culture as I (or they themselves) understand it. They have, however, proposed another (more promising) method of constructing a cultural economics.

Promoters, Peddlers and Pirates

As Lavoie and Chamlee-Wright (2000, 69) have also noted, the "spirit of enterprise comes in many different flavors." Although the entrepreneur plays the vital roles of innovation and coordination within all markets, the ideal-typical entrepreneur may differ considerably across time and place. Context does matter. And, because entrepreneurs from different cultures operate on the basis of different primary metaphors and posses different models of entrepreneurial success, the "quintessential entrepreneur would be described as having different qualities" in different contexts (ibid.).

The Japanese entrepreneur, for instance, typically operates his firm as a father would his family or a coach/team-captain would his team.[18] Corporate unity is stressed and employees are expected to subordinate their individual identities to the team. Compare this with the "entrepreneurial pattern" that emerges in more individualistic cultures where entrepreneurs are typically thought of as cowboys or mavericks. Correspondingly, the British entrepreneur at the time of the industrial revolution and the contemporary Jamaican haggler while sharing many similarities (a *spirit of enterprise* infects both characters) also differ from each other in many respects. The haggler, for example, is less likely to expect that her activities will be translated into real material success and her opportunities and avenues for attaining capital and credit will also differ.[19]

"Each culture," Lavoie and Chamlee-Wright (ibid.) point out, "creates a unique entrepreneurial pattern; each culture articulates its own genre of stories in which economic leaders achieve wealth-generating success within the specific institutional and customary contours of the society in which they live." It is not that entrepreneurs exploit their society's cultural advantages or utilize its cultural strengths, as Lavoie and Chamlee-Wright sometimes seem to be suggesting, but instead that they correctly "read" and "interpret" the opportunities to profit and the avenues to economic success particular to their context. Culture, as Chamelee-Wright (1997, 49) has reminded us, "provides the framework within which entrepreneurs not only notice, but also creatively piece together profit opportunities from the world around them." And, as I have cited before, "the seeing of profit opportunities is a matter of cultural interpretation" (Lavoie 1991, 36). What Lavoie and Chamlee-Wright recommend, therefore, is that we pay attention to, that we *appreciate,* "the rich diversity of these narratives" (ibid.) if we intend to understand entrepreneurship within its context. How do we do this? How do we contextualize the entrepreneur? How do we give the cultural muscles and flesh that they are calling for to the skeleton of the entrepreneur developed by Kirzner and others? Both separately and together Lavoie (1991, 1994) and Chamlee-Wright (1994, 1997; and 2001 with Lavoie) have given us several well developed hints as to the path they suggest.

What they propose is (ultimately) that we shift our focus from the entrepreneurial function and, instead, pay attention to entrepreneurs. That we, as they put it, find out which stories are told in her community, the myths that are widely shared and believed by her fellows, the heroes that are admired and the metaphors that are used in her context (Lavoie and Chamlee-Wright 2000, 52). We should, as they have suggested, focus on the ideal-typical, the quintessential entrepreneurs in particular cultures; the Ghanaian market woman and the Harare market woman that Chamlee-Wright (1997, 2000a, 2000b) has so adroitly described in her applied work are both classic examples of this method.

I should note at this stage that Lavoie and Chamlee-Wright's proposal that we focus on the entrepreneurial form in addition to looking at the essential nature of the entrepreneurial function is not unique to them. Mises (1949, 254), for instance, just over a half century before Lavoie and Chamlee-Wright, conceded that economics (particularly its descriptive and historical branches) cannot do without the entrepreneur as both an ideal type and an economic category. The entrepreneurs of pure economic theory, he notes, "are not living men as one meets them in the reality of life and history. [Rather,] they are the embodiment of distinct functions in the market operations" (ibid., 253). But, Mises asserted later on, there is another way in which economics "always did and still does" use the term, that is, to designate an ideal type. Economics "calls entrepreneurs those who are especially eager to profit from adjusting production to the expected changes in conditions, those who have more initiative, more venturesomeness, and a quicker eye than the crowd, the pushing and promoting pioneers of economic improvement" (ibid., 255).

Mises (ibid.) recommended that we call this *entrepreneur qua ideal type* a promoter (to avoid confusion) and argued that,

> Economics cannot do without the promoter concept. For it refers to a datum that is a general characteristic of human nature, that is present in all market transactions and marks them profoundly. This is the fact that various individuals do not react to a change in conditions with the same quickness and in the same way. The inequality of men, which is due to differences both in their inborn qualities and in the vicissitudes of their lives, manifests itself in this way.

Promoters are an essential part of the market process and "how they play that part" is subsequently of interest to economists. Presumably, like other men, the ends they desire and the means they employ are suggested to them by their cultures. As Mises (1949, 46) asserts, "inheritance and environment directs a man's actions; . . . he lives as a man of his people."

Lavoie and Chamlee-Wright's program is thus entirely consistent with the program proposed by Mises (again almost a half a century before) and their recommendation that we pay attention to *entrepreneurs qua ideal types* (particularly if we're engaged in descriptive economics or economic history) should be seen as part of Mises' (and Weber's) project. The peddlers that Geertz found in Modjokuto and described in *Peddlers and Princes* (1963) are, therefore, representative of the embedded entrepreneur that Lavoie and Chamlee-Wright have proposed we look at.

Remember, "Modjokutu from its beginning has had a bazaar economy" peopled with a large number of "highly competitive commodity traders who relate to one another mainly by means of an incredible volume of *ad hoc* acts of exchange" (Geertz 1963, 29). Geertz describes these peddlers in graphic detail. They are determined, innovative and driven characters who are opportunistic, perhaps to their detriment. The Modjokutu peddler is an "entrepreneur without an enterprise" who is not interested in reducing his cost of doing business but is instead focused on "petty speculation" (ibid.). He does not or, as Geertz asserts, is unable to "search out and create new sources of profit." Instead, he merely grasps "occasions for gain as they fitfully and, from his point of view, spontaneously arise" (ibid.). As discussed earlier, the history of Modjokutu and the peculiar structure (at least for Java) of the Modjokutu township (for instance, the absence of a significant landed gentry) has given rise to this particular entrepreneurial culture and has created the Modjokutu peddler.

Another character that I contend is consistent with Lavoie and Chamlee-Wright's embedded entrepreneur is the Bahamian *master pirate*. The most successful industries in the Bahamas' economic story have been pirate-like in character. Whether they were pirates, or ship-wreckers, or blockade runners, or rum smugglers, or drug dealers, or even off-shore bankers, many of the entrepreneurs that appear in the Bahamian economic narrative were engaged in activities that were morally dubious at best. The Bahamas' economic past, I contend, has given rise to an entrepreneur that is alert to opportunities to profiteer rather than profit. In the next two chapters, I attempt to describe and develop this ideal type of the *master pirate* as well as the ideal-type of the *enterprising slave*, the other figure that I contend is an important part of the economic story of the Bahamas.

Notes

[1] As Lachmann (1977, 94) asserts, "In reading [Mises' Human Action (1949)] we must never forget that it is the work of Max Weber that is being carried on here."

[2] It should be noted, however, that the polity, the state, was largely absent from Granovetter's arguments.

[3] Weber, however, did at least hint at the importance cultural studies in his social economics. "The quality of an event as a 'social-economic' event," he contends, "is not something which it possesses 'objectively.' It is rather conditioned by the orientation of our interest of understanding, as it arises from the specific cultural significance which we attribute to the particular event in a given case" (Weber [1949] 1997, 64).

[4] This study, similarly, can be read as arguing that in the Bahamas, two competing metaphors of entrepreneurship – *business as piracy* and *business as enterprise* – are at work. As noted in the introduction, *Chapters 3 (piracy)* and *4 (enterprise)* trace the evolution of those two metaphors and *Chapter 5* traces the way these metaphors affect contemporary business practices. The arguments of this project, thus, closely parallel Bird-David's work on the Nayaka.

[5] As Gudeman (2001, 34) describes, "Around the world, many constructions of the commons [the natural environment] and its connection to people are found. But in countless instances, the base [that is, the underlying economic reality] of a group is modeled as part of community itself, not as a separate, mechanically driven object, as in the Newtonian construct of capital. Such cultural models do not distinguish between the human and nonhuman constituents of community, or between people and material; the social, spiritual, and material sustenance of the community are one."

[6] As Lipset (1990, 129) reports, "a 1984 study by the Ontario Securities Commission reports that four-fifths of the companies on the Toronto Stock Exchange's 300 Index are controlled by seven families. Crossnational data reveal that Canada's 32 wealthiest families plus five conglomerates 'control about one-third of the country's non-financial assets. . . . By comparison, in the U.S. the 100 largest firms, few of which are controlled by individuals, own one-third of the non-financial assets.' Only 15 percent of the 500 companies on the American Standard and Poor's stock index have a large stockholder; in Canada, at least one-quarter of the stock in 93 percent of the country's largest publicly held corporations 'is held by a family or conglomerate.' While the United States has literally thousands of small banks, Canada's five largest chartered banks almost totally dominate the industry in their country, holding 80 percent of all deposits; another five have an additional 10 percent."

[7] As Geertz (2000, 65) remarked, the principle objection to the claim that *culture does not matter* "is not that it rejects an it's-all-how-you-look-at-it approach to knowledge or a when-in-Rome approach to morality, but that it imagines that they can only be defeated by placing morality beyond culture and knowledge beyond both. This,

speaking of things which must needs be so, is no longer possible. If we wanted home truths, we should have stayed at home." Like Geertz, I simply believe that context makes a difference.

[8] As we shall see (*Chapter* 4), the decline of the plantation economy in the Bahamas had a similar effect on economic activities in that context. The death of the cotton plantations meant the birth of the *enterprising slave.*

[9] As North (1994, 364) remarked, "The current learning of any generation takes place within the context of the perceptions derived from collective learning. Learning then is an incremental process filtered by the culture of a society."

[10] High (1990) summarizes quite succinctly the implications of assuming omniscient actors, as is done by mainstream economists. As High (ibid., 51) suggests, when "the set of possible alternatives from which [a maximizer] chooses is assumed to be comprehensive," then "his attempt to achieve the most desirable of these opportunities always succeeds." There would be no need for entrepreneurship in that context.

[11] It is important to note that these "spheres of ignorance" are at the same time evidence that the economy is in disequilibrium and that there are opportunities to capture profits (see High 1990). The former point is an important one but, since it is not necessary for me to pursue this claim for this current effort, it will not be developed here. Instead, I will turn my attention to the latter point regarding the opportunity for entrepreneurial profits given our fundamental ignorance, and focus on their role in entrepreneurial efforts. See Kirzner (1973) for a discussion of the equilibrating nature of the entrepreneur. See Lavoie (1991) and Schumpeter ([1934], 1983) for an alternate view.

[12] As High (1990, 54) argued, "uncertainty introduces a mental operation into choice that is absent from maximizing subject to known constraints. A person who does not know all the various influences that will determine an outcome, or who does not know the strength of the various influences, must exercise judgment." Pointing out that "alertness is also important in uncertain situations," High (ibid.) argues that "by being alert to the various influences that will determine an outcome, one can improve one's judgment. Similarly, by being alert to information that indicates how strong the various influences will be, a person can make better judgments. Obviously, those in the market who are able to judge uncertain situations better than others will profit."

[13] As Gadamer (1976, 71) remarks, "in general, we are not at all ready to hear things in their own being," instead "they are [first] subjected to man's calculus." Hayek has made a similar point. As he (1948, 63) suggests, "If we consider for a moment the simplest kinds of actions where this problem arises, it becomes, of course, rapidly obvious that, in discussing what we regard as other people's conscious actions, we invariably interpret their action on the analogy of our own mind: that is, that we group their actions, and the objects of their actions, into classes or categories which we know solely from the knowledge of our own mind. We assume that the idea of a

purpose or a tool, a weapon or food, is common to them with us, just as we assume that they can see the difference between different colors or shapes as well as we. We thus always supplement what we actually see of another person's action by projecting into that person a system of classification of objects which we know, not from observing other people, but because it is in terms of these classes that we think ourselves. If, for example, we watch a person cross a square full of traffic, dodging some cars and pausing to let others pass, we know (or we believe we know) much more than we actually perceive with our eyes. This would be equally true if we saw a man behave in a physical environment quite unlike anything we have ever seen before. If I see for the first time a big boulder or an avalanche coming down the side of a mountain toward a man and see him run for his life, I know the meaning of this action because I know what I would or might have done in similar circumstances."

[14] Indeed, Kirzner would likely have agreed with Coppin and High's (1999, 12) assertion that "the bureaucratic entrepreneur is no less a force of American life than the business entrepreneur." As Coppin and High's (1999, 11) suggest, "Enterprising bureaucrats have changed American social life. They have influenced the food we eat, the clothes we wear, the environment we work in, the schools our children attend, the terms we trade on, and our political process. They have built huge organizations with budgets that run into the hundreds of millions of dollars and with control over land, labor, and capital that rival the resources of successful business leaders." While entrepreneurs in a market context generally seek to maximize their profits, they argue, "bureaucratic entrepreneurs are appointed government officials who exercise creativity, alertness, judgment, and persuasion in attempting to increase their control over scarce [public] resources" (Coppin and High 1999, 13).

[15] This is not to say that cultures are immutable. To be sure, cultural beliefs, practices, values, ideals, symbols, meanings, etc. (though not in flux) are constantly evolving and adapting. New artifacts are continually being produced that are beyond replicas of existing artifacts. New "texts" are continually being written. Although cultural systems are changeable, however, they are not fungible. Even the so-called 'Cultural Revolution' in China (and its attending violence) – which (arguably) aimed at destroying traditional Chinese culture and replacing it with Maoism – really only succeeded at destroying Chinese cultural artifacts. Similarly, though francophone colonialism was a brutal attempt at cultural imperialism, it failed to transform the Algerians or the Vietnamese into little Frenchman.

[16] See Arrow (2000) for a similar critique of social capital.

[17] As Lachmann (1977, 62) says of institutions, "there also are certain superindividual schemes of thought, namely, *institutions*, to which the schemes of thought of the first order, the plans, must be oriented, and which serve therefore, to some extent, the coordination of individual plans. They constitute, we may say, 'interpersonal orientation tables,' schemes of thought of the second order."

[18] See Trompenaars and Hampden-Turner (1997).

[19] And, as Baumol (1990, 894) suggests, although "entrepreneurs are always with us and always play *some* substantial role . . . there are a variety of roles among which the entrepreneur's efforts can be reallocated, and some of those roles do not follow the constructive and innovative script that is conventionally attributed to that person . . . How the entrepreneur acts at a given time and place depends heavily on the rules of the game – the reward structure in the economy – that happen to prevail." Those rules, I should add, are necessarily filtered through each entrepreneur's cultural lens.

Chapter Three

Expulsis Piratis: Piracy as a Model and Metaphor for Economic Success

Introduction

By almost any standard the Bahamas is a beautiful country. The evidence is overwhelming. In the water just off the coast of Paradise Island near Nassau, schools of tiny silver fish with orange-gold tails and thick black streaks along their bodies swim just beneath the ocean's surface easily perceptible in the crystal clear sea water. On beaches lined with coconut trees and partially sheltered by palm branches, footprints crisscross in pearl colored sand until they are swallowed up by waves that lazily roll ashore. On the day after Christmas and again on New Years day, Bahamians and their guests from all over the planet take to the streets to witness and participate in one of the most frantic celebrations ever. Revelers wear bright multi-colored costumes made of crepe paper and cardboard, beat out rhythms reminiscent of African rhythms on goat skin drums and shake cowbells creating a sight and sound that is thoroughly enjoyed by all and not easily forgotten. The sun shines constantly in the Bahamas as do the people; almost everyone who visits the Bahamas comments on how warm and friendly Bahamians tend to be. The only unattractive feature of this nation of islands seems to be its history. Particularly, its economic history.

The Bahamas has suffered successive periods of dramatic, momentary booms followed by equally dramatic but protracted busts. The riches from blockade running during the American Civil War, for instance, evaporated just as soon as the war ended and the Bahamas remained a "depressed" area until American Prohibition presented visitors and citizens alike with another smuggling opportunity. Besides this pattern of short booms and long busts, another theme permeates Bahamian economic history: the *pirate character* of successful industries. This, however, should not be surprising.

Indeed, any history of the Bahamas would be incomplete without recounting its history of piracy; without reminding us of Blackbeard, of Ann Bonney, of Governor Rogers, of Calico Jack; without mentioning the "Jolly Roger," the skull and crossbones, the tales of daring, the canon fire; without pointing out the similarities between piracy, privateering, ship wrecking, blockade running, rum running, drug smuggling and even off-shore banking; in short, without pointing out that all of the Bahamas' successful industries save tourism (and even there the record is unclear, see *Chapter 5*) are very similar in nature to buccaneering. Indeed, privateering was simply state-sanctioned piracy. To the victims of Henry Morgan when he was regarded by the British as a notorious pirate and the victims of the "legitimated" Henry Morgan of latter years who served as a privateer, the distinction between pirates and privateers must have seemed dubious, at best. "A privateer," as Cordingly (1995, xvii) informs us, "was [simply] an armed vessel, or the commander and crew of that vessel, which was licensed to attack and seize the vessels of a hostile nation;" both pirates and privateers attacked and plundered merchant ships. Similarly, wrecking involved luring unsuspecting ships to their ruin on the coral reefs that surround the Bahama Islands and "salvaging" their cargo. And, gun running, rum running and drug dealing, all required that their participants flout if not domestic laws then certainly the laws of a neighboring country. To be sure, the laws of a neighboring country are not *ipso facto* sacrosanct. Countries sometimes have very unjust laws (slavery, for instance, was legally sanctioned for much of the world's history). But, extra-legal activities are not simply accepted in the Bahamas, they are encouraged by and celebrated in Bahamian culture and, at various times, they have sustained the Bahamian economy. Consequently, it is possible to think of the story of the Bahamas as a story about the survival of piracy. And, it is clear from even a cursory read of the Bahamas' economic history that piracy has been a consistent theme.[1]

Piracy as a Way of Doing Business

Others have pointed out these "similarities" between piracy (in its 17th century variety) and other successful industries in the Bahamas. Strachan (1995, 191) in his important commentary *Paradise and Plantation: The Economy of Caribbean Discourse* (1995), for instance, has characterized "wrecking, blockade running during the American Civil War, and bootlegging in the 1920s" as "'piratical' enterprises." Similarly, Craton and Saunders (1992, 114) in their comprehensive history of the Bahamas have argued that "piracy and its milder correlatives— privateering, wrecking, smuggling, running blockades — . . . provided a perennial, or at least recurrent, factor in the shaping of Bahamian life and character." As they asserted, "poverty, lack of resources, and the heartbreaking drudgery of alternative occupations meant that Bahamians would recurrently be tempted by the chance of instant or easy riches, irrespective of legal prohibitions or abstract morality" (ibid.). Piracy has been a definite model for economic success in the Bahamas ever since the 17th century, when Nassau on Providence Island (now New Providence) was a favorite harbor for West Indian pirates.

Piratical Enterprises: A History of Booms in the Bahamas

During the last years of the seventeenth century and the first two decades of the eighteenth, the Bahamas was a "nest of pirates." As Lane (1998, 188) confirms, "the Bahamas attracted hundreds, and perhaps even thousands of pirates between 1716 and 1718." It is clear, for instance, that beginning in 1680s the Bahamas was "fast becoming the Anglo-American pirate base of choice" (not just one of a variety of alternatives) and as "many of the 5000 pirates active in American waters between 1716 and 1726. . . stopped at the Bahamas to careen, carouse, sell stolen goods, and plan new exploits" (ibid.). As *The Pirates Own Book* (1837, 358) explains,[2]

> The Bahamas, themselves are a singular group of isles, reefs and quays; consisting of several hundred in number, and were the chief resort of pirates in old times . . . they are low and not elevated, and are more than 600 miles in extent, cut up into numerous intricate passages and channels, full of sunken rocks and coral reefs. They afforded a sure retreat to desperadoes.

In fact, the Island of Providence (now New Providence), a relatively small island (only seven by twenty-one miles), located in the center of the Bahamian archipelago and tucked in between Eleuthera (to the east) and Andros (to the west), was particularly suited to act as a pirate headquarters. As Black (1989, 12) contends,

> The Bahamas, with its nest of countless islands, cays and reefs, was the ideal base from which to pounce on merchantmen making their way through the Windward Passage or Florida Channel. So it was here, in the early 1690s, with their headquarters at New Providence (the Nassau of today), that the English pirates set up their commonwealth – successor to the buccaneer's Tortuga, and miniature Madagascar of the West.

The harbor at Nassau (the Bahamas' capital city) was large enough for 500 ships and the island was "strategically located" along the profitable shipping lanes between North America and the Americas (Craton and Saunders 1992, 108). Today cruise liners on their way to and from the Americas rather than pirate sloops fill Nassau harbor, but it was from this (still) optimally located harbor city that dozens of ships sailing under the black flag, attacked and plundered British, Spanish and French vessels laden with gold and other trade goods.[3]

Admittedly, it is difficult to get a precise measure of how successful the pirates based in the Bahamas were or the degree of damage that they did to trade in the region. But, the body of circumstantial evidence suggests that the Bahamian based pirates were wildly successful and that their deleterious impact on trade was substantial. Based in the Bahamas during this era were perhaps the most infamous and notorious pirates found anywhere in any epoch. The "lady pirates" Anne Bonney and Mary Reed were headquartered in the Bahamas. As was the daredevil Calico Jack, Captain Jennings, Charles Vane and the ignoble Edward Teach, a.k.a. Blackbeard. Similarly, dispatches from governors throughout the Americas to King George I and to each other repeatedly complained about the Bahamas' pirate problem (Craton [1962] 1986, 92).[4] And, a 1717 report from the Council of Trade and Plantations to Secretary Addison (who served in the King's cabinet) warned that there was nothing in place to stop the islands from being "plundered and ravaged by pirates" and that the Bahamas was "in danger of being lost from Our Crown of Great Britain" (cited in Cordingly 1995, 151).

New Providence, however, was not only the base from which the West Indian pirates planned and launched their attacks, it was also the port where they went when they were rich with booty to spend their spoils. As is often remarked, pirates were the Bahamas' first stopover tourists. Recall that the pirates of that era, "stopped at the Bahamas to careen, carouse, [and] sell stolen goods" (Lane 1998, 188). As Black (1989, 12) describes, "with its influx of traders, merchants and prostitutes, West Indian piracy was to flourish here until the 1720s when Britain finally established a settled government over the islands." As such, the local Bahamian economy was able to benefit quite a bit from the large bounties that accompanied the pirates as they returned from their voyages. Craton ([1962] 1986), for instance, has called this period one of the most prosperous periods in the history of the Bahamas. The sea-roving pirates of the Blackbeard era, however, were eventually suppressed. Although the 1718 appointment of Woodes Rogers as Governor of the Bahama Islands meant an end to piracy in the colony, almost as soon as they were expelled from the Bahamian waters, "piracy" again became a dominant industry in the Bahamas (albeit now in another guise); with mostly land based *wreckers* replacing the seafaring *corsairs*.

Craton ([1962] 1986, 166) has fittingly called *wrecking* the Bahamas' perennial standby industry. Whenever there was a downturn in other economic activities (for instance, the suppression of piracy, the decline of sisal production or the collapse of the plantation economy), Bahamians turned to *wrecking* for their subsistence. Well into the 19th century, the sea could be counted on to cough up more than the occasional prize. In the late 1700s and the early 1800s, the popular trade routes between North America and the Americas continued to pass through the uncharted, shallow waters of the Bahamas. Not surprisingly, then, ships filled with trade goods frequently crashed into the Bahamas' nefarious coral reefs. At various times in the Bahamas' past, a burgeoning industry arose around "salvaging" these wrecks, only to be supplanted, I contend, when more profitable *piratical* activities presented themselves. As Craton and Saunders (1992, 87) assert, "each year, unwary or unfortunate navigators on their way to and from the Caribbean added to the toll of Bahamian shoals and reefs, and even the wrecks of small freighting vessels carrying out provisions or carrying back produce could yield more returns than years of labor ashore."

To call what the *wreckers* did "salvaging," however, would be a gross misrepresentation. This was no humanitarian effort to help the captain and crew of a sinking ship save what could be saved from the damaged vessel. But was instead, at its best, an attempt to benefit from the misfortune of others and, at its worst, pure theft. As one *wrecker* remarked, "I didn't go there for humanity: I went *racking*" (Craton ([1962] 1986, 167). Ships were not warned that they were approaching dangerous areas (often they were lured into those areas) and, in the scramble for *wreck* goods after a crash, the *wreckers* showed little regard for the welfare of the sinking ship's passengers and crew. As Johnson (1972, 7) reports, "the ingenious islanders soon discovered that their gains could be made more certain if they gave a helpful nudge to chance by deliberately lighting the way of hapless ships towards the treacherous reefs." The chronicler Oldmixon offers a similar description in his *History of the Isle of Providence* (1708),

> As for Wrecks, the People of Providence, Harbour-Island and Eleuthera, dealt in them as it is said the good men of Sussex do: All that came ashore Prize, and if a Sailor had, by better Luck than the rest, got ashore as well as his Wreck, he was not sure of getting off again as well. This perhaps is Scandal, but it is most notorious, that the Inhabitants looked upon every Thing they could get out of a Cast-away Ship as their own, and were not at any Trouble to enquire after the Owners. [cited in Riley (1983, 45)]

Dr. Townsend's account of his visit to the islands in 1823 is strikingly similar to Oldmixon's. Arguing that *wrecking* is simply piracy with a new face, Dr. Townsend writes,

> It is affirmed that Nassau was first settled by a colony of pirates under the celebrated Blackbeard. Smuggling and wrecking as they are practiced in these islands are next-a-kin to piracy or no better than a refined species of it. The Bahamians are very expert and adroit at it, it is said, perhaps owing to a hereditary predisposition and tact, for if tradition is to be believed all the inhabitants are either lineally or collaterally descended from the founder of Nassau & his associates. [cited in Craton & Saunders (1992, 250)]

Indeed, for much of the Bahamas' history, *wrecking* was big business (the government licensed wreckers and taxed wreck goods).[5] At the industry's height in the 1850s, wreck goods comprised over two-thirds of the colony's exports and nearly half of the able-bodied men in the colony were engaged in wrecking.[6]

Running the blockade during the American Civil War and rum smuggling during the American experiment with Prohibition, however, promised to be and were ultimately far more lucrative than wrecking ever was.[7] Almost as soon as the Union Navy began blockading Confederate ports, for instance, ships loaded with needed wares began setting sail from the Bahamas, attempting to smuggle guns and manufactures past the blockading vessels. These efforts at smuggling were overwhelmingly successful and this enterprise proved to be a real boon to the Bahamian economy (resembling the piracy generated boom some decades before). As Albury (1975, 153) asserted, "in Nassau [during the American Civil War], money flowed like water." And, as he (ibid.) continued later,

> Shops and warehouses sprouted up as fast as they could be built. And they were all filled to the ceiling before the last nail was driven. Fortunes, which ordinarily could not be accumulated in a lifetime, were made in a few weeks.
>
> Captains, pilots and sailors of the blockade runners found it impossible to spend, or even squander, all the money they made.

The profits made from blockade running far outstretched those made or hoped for by either wreckers or pirates. As Saunders (1990, 87) reports, "For the Bahamas, blockade-running increased trade significantly. As a result, the value of imports went up from 274,584 pounds sterling in 1861 to 1,250,322 pounds sterling in 1862, and the value of exports from 195,584 pounds sterling to over 1 million pounds sterling over the same period."

Rum smuggling was a similar boon to the Bahamian economy. On January 15, 1920 it became illegal in the United States of America to sell, manufacture or transport intoxicating beverages. American gangsters responded by establishing *speakeasies* and foreign producers of alcoholic beverages, in turn, began looking for ways to get their products (illegally) onto American soil. The Bahamas, once again, became a center for smuggling "contraband" into North America. Once again, Bahamian entrepreneurs were enlisted in illicit enterprises. And, once again, the Bahamian economy boomed. Government revenue from import licenses, for instance, doing the period quadrupled just two years after Prohibition was enacted (Albury 1975, 180).[8]

Admittedly, the "increase in commerce" from smuggling guns and rum was neither theft nor quasi-theft like privateering, piracy and wrecking but was basic "run of the mill" trade entered into voluntarily. In fact, a case can be made that the Union Navy or United States law enforcement agencies were the pirates in these particular plots. Still, there is something that links blockade running and rum smuggling (and their cousin drug smuggling) with *wrecking* and *piracy*. There is a similar willingness to directly oppose foreign powers and to flout foreign laws that characterizes all these industries and, like piracy, these industries were very risky and yielded hefty returns in a hurry. Also, like piracy these industries were primarily extractive (rather than productive).[9] Smugglers are essentially extracting the artificial rents created by oppressive (highly restrictive) trade policies. If prohibition did not exist, for example, the Bahamas would not have become a major transshipment point for alcohol nor would Bahamian smugglers be significant players in the trade of goods between American consumers and British and other European producers.[10]

That these industries were the successful (even the most successful enterprises) in Bahamian history is not, however, sufficient to explain why piracy became the dominant model for attaining economic success in the Bahamas. Indeed, the Bahamas did not and does not have a monopoly on piratical enterprises. Other pirate havens, however, I contend, can not boast of the same parade of "piratical" enterprises. Cuba, for instance, was also a "nest of pirates" and in the Havana of the 1820s "piracy [was] as much tolerated there as any profession" (Marine Research Society 1837, 360). But, there were alternate sources of wealth in Cuba. Tobacco and sugar plantations thrived in Cuba and Havana (Cuba's capital city) was a major mercantile center in the nineteenth century even when piracy was at its peak there. As we shall see, the Bahamas' experience with piracy was a unique one: in the Bahamas the viable alternatives to piratical enterprises simply did not exist.

The Uniqueness of the Bahamas' Pirate Narrative

I have already catalogued the Bahamian experience with piratical enterprises. Recall that for much of the 17th century and the first few decades of the 18th century, the Bahamas was a den of pirates. The most notorious pirates of that era used the Bahamas as a base of operations; Captains Jennings, Hornigold, Vane and Teach were all based in Providence Island. From Nassau's natural harbor, these pirates launched their fleets of (often) three or four ships to attack and plunder. Nassau, however, was not only a staging area; it was also a popular pirate rendezvous. After a successful expedition it was common for pirates rich with Spanish pieces-of-eight and other booty to return to the Bahamas to *carouse*, sell their wares and plan new voyages. Indeed, the infamy of the Bahamian based pirates alone might be sufficient to explain why piracy has evolved as a model for business in the Bahamas. Bahamians believe that Blackbeard and his contemporaries were successful and that belief alone is sufficient to affect our models. Worldviews, as I have argued, are subjective.[11] But, with Governor Rogers arrival in 1718, Nassau would no longer be a safe harbor for pirates, however infamous. Why did piracy evolve as a dominant model for attaining economic success in the Bahamas?

To be sure, Woodes Rogers, a former privateer, was appointed Governor of the Bahamas in February 1718 and by December of that year "he had successfully taken and transformed the greatest pirate den in the world" (Albury 1975, 75). Rogers commemorated his accomplishment with a new, hopeful motto for the colony: *Expulsis Piratis – Restituta Commercia*, Pirates Expelled – Commerce Restored. This was to be the colony's motto until 1973 when it was granted independence from Britain. But, I contend, the sentiment expressed in Rogers' motto was less real than it was apparent. Ironically, the pirates were never expelled from the Bahamian waters, one form of piracy was illegitimated but, as we have seen, others thrived. Similarly, commerce was never really restored to the Bahamas (the popular trade routes of the day were no longer frustrated by Bahamian based pirates but the Bahamas never became an agricultural or mercantile center). It is both this failure to live up to the sentiments expressed in Roger's motto and the salient features of piracy as practiced during the Blackbeard era (as opposed to say the Barbary Coast or the Spanish *corsair* variations) that explains how piracy evolved as a way of doing business in the Bahamas.

As I have argued, when Roger's expelled the seafaring pirates from the Bahamas, commerce was not restored. Indeed, with the possible exception of tourism (which I will discuss in depth in *Chapter 5*), no non-piratical enterprise has thrived in the Bahamas. Industries like sponging, fisheries, woodcutting, salting and searching for ambergris and seal oil have been important economic activities in the

Bahamas ever since the Eleutherian Adventurers (the first group of European settlers) came to the colony. Because these are primarily extractive activities, however, any success that Bahamian entrepreneurs have had with them has been both limited and short-lived.[12]

Unfortunately, the same can be said for their experience with agriculture; because of the country's poor soil, agriculture has never really been a viable enterprise in the Bahamas.[13] Although cotton, tomatoes and pineapples have at one time or another been important cash crops in the Bahamas, the Bahamian soils have proved to be easily exhausted. Settlers and citizens often found that in spite of their early successes with this or that crop, they were eventually unable to compete in foreign markets or with foreign producers in domestic markets on either quality or cost. At the height of the *cotton boom* (1785 – 1788), for instance, much of the southern Bahamas (about 8,000 acres) was under cotton production (Johnson 1996, 10). As Craton ([1962] 1986, 156) reports, "by the end of 1785, 2,476 acres had been planted and 124 tons were exported. In 1786 this increased to 150 tons from 2,050 acres and in 1787, 219 tons were produced from 4,500 acres, for a total value of £27,393." However, 1789 would prove to be the beginning of the end of the cotton industry in the Bahamas. That was the year the chenille caterpillar began attacking Bahamian crops. As Johnson (1996, 26) informs, "the effect of insect pests was partly responsible for the slump in cotton exports to 3,000 pounds in 1794 and 1,800 pounds in 1797." Notice that this is over a 99% decline in the industry in ten years. Hurricanes also adversely affected the industry but by all accounts the soil was the main culprit (see, for instance, McKinnen 1804). Bahamian soils are "thin, scattered, and easily exhausted" and were, thus, never suited for the production of cotton (Craton and Saunders 1992, 196). As Johnson (1996, 28) notes, "Although cotton was cultivated on a small scale as late as the 1830s, the commercial industry barely survived the eighteenth century."

Agriculture, however, has thrived in many of the other *pirate paradises.* I mentioned Cuba and its continued success with both sugar and tobacco cultivation before. Compare also the Bahamas' experience with agriculture (cotton production, as well as, tomato and pineapple production which have had similar histories), for instance, with the Malagasy experience. Madagascar became pirate port of choice after the British Empire began cracking down on piracy in the West Indies. Madagascar was strategically located along the European trade routes with the Far East. From Île Saine Marie and other bases on the east coast, Madagascar based pirates (like Captain Avery) set out to ambush ships laden with cargo as they passed around the Cape of Good Hope. Although piracy was as entrenched in Madagascar as it was in the Bahamas, the Malagasy have also benefited considerably from other activities; sugar, rice, vanilla and cotton have all been profitable export crops. A similar point could be made about the other pirate havens of that era. Jamaica, for example, has had (and continues to have) success with a number of non-piratical industries (particularly sugar).

Of course, I am not suggesting that piracy does not exist as a model for doing business in these other *pirate ports*. In fact, that corruption has plagued Madagascar, Jamaica and Cuba suggests that all three contexts have (at least to some extent) evolved pirate cultures. What I am suggesting, however, is that the absence of viable alternatives to piratical enterprises explains how piracy evolved as such a dominant way of doing business in the Bahamas. Unlike their cousins in the other *pirate paradises*, Bahamian entrepreneurs were not presented with the same range of competing models of economic success. In addition, piracy as practiced in the Bahamas was perhaps more readily appropriated as a model of entrepreneurship than the kinds of piracy that evolved in other contexts.

The famed Barbary corsairs who attacked Spanish galleons and cities in the Mediterranean from their bases in Algiers, for instance, had very little in common with the swashbuckling pirates that frequented Nassau, Port Royal and Tortuga. The Barbary corsairs were more mercenaries than muggers. Early in the 16th century, King Ferdinand launched several efforts to conquer the Barbary (in reality "Berber") Coast in North Africa for Spain. The so-called Barbary pirates were part and parcel of the Turkish Ottoman Empire's resistance efforts. These corsairs not only frustrated merchant shipping but also attacked and attempted to capture Spanish soldiers, fleets and cities. Oruç's greatest victory, for instance, was his "annihilation" of "a fleet carrying 7,000 veteran Spanish soldiers sent to relieve the fort of El Peñón in 1517" (Lane 1998, 13). Similarly, (Oruç's younger brother) Hayreddin's most famous campaign was when he "finally drove the Spanish from their fortress at El Peñón in 1529" (ibid.).[14] The Barbary corsairs were not the independent, sea-roving bandits that operated out of the Bahamas in the early 1700s but were, instead, soldiers fighting a war. As Lane (1998, 202) summarizes, "what the Spanish universally called piracy was in this earlier stage more often privateering. Home governments, however weak, usually condoned rather than decried the predatory acts of their subjects abroad."

It is hard to imagine Algerians maintaining piracy as practiced off the Berber Coast as a model of entrepreneurship (perhaps it can be seen as a model for defense or obtaining power or as a geo-political weapon but not as a path to economic success). The Barbary corsairs like the French corsairs of the sixteenth century were led by aristocrats and petty nobles, their crews were organized hierarchically and the loot won by these vessels were not distributed democratically. In fact, the Barbary corsairs typically operated galleys rowed by slaves (Cordingly 1995, 158). Piracy (or more accurately privateering) was not the way for the typical Algerian to gain economic success. But, as Lane (1998, 203) informs, the pirates of the Blackbeard era (the ones likely to frequent the Bahamas) "were self-governing, near egalitarian, conscientious of the welfare of their fellows and more interested in great times than great titles. In short, they actively rejected the rigid class biases then entrenched in Europe and self-consciously mimicked in the colonies." These pirates, Lane (ibid.) continues, "mocked European conventions of estate, sexuality, religious authority, and judicial process, and on occasion even disregarded . . . the colour and gender prejudices of their day."[15] Piracy was a path to greater prosperity for rich and poor, male and female, black and white, former noblemen and former slaves alike.

That this variant of piracy (open to all and focused on *profits rather than conquest*) became a dominant model of entrepreneurship in the Bahamas becomes readily understandable when we consider the effect that the past has on the present. As I have argued elsewhere, there is a certain path dependence to development experiences (Storr 2002). People learn from their pasts; it alerts them to one set of opportunities and, often, blinds them to other possibilities. History, I contend, seems to be telling Bahamian entrepreneurs that the most profitable enterprises (indeed the only profitable enterprises) all resemble piracy in one form or another. While wrecking and smuggling activities have repeatedly proven to be profitable enterprises in the Bahamas, for instance, the repeated failures of agricultural efforts has made farming seem like a foolish endeavor. This lesson, poignant and problematic, has even colored those ventures that are not in and of themselves piratical enterprises.

Piracy as a Metaphor for Business

That piracy is a viable model of business success, however, is not only a lesson that is taught by the Bahamas' economic history. It is also a view transmitted (and even encouraged) by Bahamian culture. The subtle differences in the corporate cultures that dominate Bahamian workplaces and say American work spaces is quite illustrative in this regard. The employee who walks to work in gym shoes and changes into business shoes once she reaches the office is a familiar scene in American corporations. It is as if she is saying with that very act 'I am here now' and 'I have come to give a full days work for a full days pay.' The familiar scene in Bahamian office spaces sends precisely the opposite message. The Bahamian worker comes into work fully adorned in business attire; her shoes, her briefcase and her business suit all suggest that she is a serious worker. But when she gets to work she undertakes a transformation. She removes her business shoes and puts on a pair of bedroom slippers that she has bought to wear around the office. It is as if she is saying with that very act, 'I am here to get a full days pay for doing as little work as possible.' That she perceived by her fellow Bahamians as a serious or at least successful worker is important to her (she wears her work shoes outside the office), but she has come to the office not to work but to relax. Indeed, the pirate as hero is a persistent theme in Bahamian *texts* and Bahamian culture often celebrates the trickster (that is, the person who gets something for nothing) while ridiculing the hard worker. This can clearly be seen in the nation's folklore.

B' Rabbi and the Bahamas' Trickster Culture

As Ogunleye (1997, 436) has taught us, for Africans both on the continent and in the Diaspora, "Folklore represents a line to a vast, interconnected network of meanings, values, and cognitions." Folktales, thus, give researchers "an invaluable framework for insight into the history and worldview" of the communities where they thrive (ibid., 435). The Bahamas, like other diasporic communities, is "rich in folklore" and was the "centre of a vibrant storytelling tradition" (Glinton 1993, 11); talking "ol' story" (both during slavery and until very recently) was an important way that Bahamians passed the time. As Glinton (ibid.,13) informs, Bahamian oral stories are typically animated productions where the storyteller is an "actor, musician and stage manager" who "makes use of mimicry (e.g. 'sperrits' always speak with a nasal voice), onomatopoeia and gestures." Also, songs are often used to "punctuate" Bahamian folk narratives. The storyteller, however, is not just an entertainer. He is also "the news-bringer and historian of the clan, prescriber and disseminator of his people's culture, upholder of their religious practices and their moral values" (Turner 1988, viii).

The preeminent figure in Bahamian folklore is B' Rabbi (the trickster). B' Rabbi and his foil B' Bouki were likely brought to the Bahamas by Africans forced to immigrate to that nation of islands in the 1600s and, as Glinton (1993, 12) describes, "are primarily a part of this country's African heritage." B' Rabbi, called Brer Rabbit in Black American communities (where he also thrived), is a "cunning" and "tricky" figure who "is the archetypal hero-trickster character" (Kulii and Kulii 2001, 46). Appearing as "Leuk, the hare and Bouki, the hyena in stories of the Wolof people of West Africa," links can also be drawn between B' Rabbi and B' Bouki and the Antillean tales of Compere Lapi or Ti Malice and Bouki (ibid.). There is also a strong affinity between B' Rabbi (or Brer Rabbit) and the "two major tricksters of Africa (Anansi or Anancy the Ashanti spider, and Ijapa, the Yoruba turtle)" (Kulii and Kulii 2001, 46). Like Anancy (which is the dominant trickster character amongst the Ashanti in Ghana as well as in the Caribbean), whether B' Rabbi is pitted against the likes of Brer Bear, Brer Wolf or Sly Brer Fox (in Black American narratives) or the powerful B' Lion and B'Whale or the dimwitted B' Bouki (his favorite adversaries in Bahamian "orature"), he "tries to nullify the plans of his [sometimes] stronger archenemies by using his superior intelligence and his quick thinking" (Kulii and Kulii 2001, 46). B' Rabbi usually gets the better of his rivals; his smarts are his chief asset and his major advantage.

Consider, for instance, the tale of *The Master Trickster*, an adaptation of a Haitian tale retold by Patricia Glinton in *An Evening in Guanima* (1993). The tale begins in the home of B' Bouki, B' Rabbi's friend and favorite foil. B' Bouki is in the kitchen with his son Lazy Borin cleaning a fish that they had stolen from an unattended fishing boat anchored at the harbor. When his scaling knife breaks, he sends his son Lazy Borin (who we learn is a "chip off the old block") to B' Rabbi to borrow another knife. As Glinton (1993, 125) informs, "Bouki's motto was 'why buy when yuh could borry [borrow].'" After some expected protest (after all he is named Lazy), Lazy Borin reluctantly sets out on his assignment. Rather than heading straight to B' Rabbi's, however, B' Bouki's son (who as we have learnt by now is "stupid, greedy and full of low cunning"), stretches "the five minute walk into a thirty-minute adventure" (Glinton 1993, 125). En route, "he stole two peach mangoes, pulled the tail of a stray goat, [and] deprived a butterfly of its wings and a lizard of its tail" (ibid.).

As he approaches Rabbi's house, however, he smells the crabs B' Rabbi is boiling for dinner and so quickens his steps; anxious to get there while there was still food to be had. When he arrived, however, "he discovered [to his dismay] that the choice dish was not yet ready for eating." B' Rabbi, in fact, had only just begun. This presented Borin with a major problem: "how does he prolong his stay at B' Rabbi's and delay his return home with the utensil he had come to borrow?" Rather than accept defeat, however, Borin contrives a way to trick B' Rabbi into letting him stay for dinner. Although not deceived by Borin's ruse ("Rabbi was after all a master trickster, while Borin was yet a babe in the trade"), B' Rabbi generously shares his dinner with the boy (who he loved like a nephew). But, B' Rabbi warned him not to tell his father. B' Rabbi had no intention, he told Borin, of feeding the two of them that evening. Of course, Borin disregarded B' Rabbi's warnings and soon after he left, Borin was back at B' Rabbi's house with his father B' Bouki, asking to share in the meal. Rabbi consented but decided to teach them a lesson.

The next day Borin appeared at B' Rabbi's door, after a similar adventure to the one he had on the day before, and asked to borrow some fire; the hearth at his father's house had gone out. While "Uncle Rab" was chastising Borin and his father for continually asking for favors, Borin, as might be expected, snuck over to the half-opened pot on the stove and saw that Rabbi was preparing boiled eggs. "Now boiled eggs to Borin and Bouki," Glinton (ibid., 130) asserts, "were like green leaves to caterpillars. However many they ate, it never seemed enough." Borin immediately began thinking of a way to share in Rabbi's meal. He decided that burning a hole through his marble bag with the slow burning stick that he had come to borrow would be the most effective. Borin timed it so that he was picking up the last marble at the same time that B' Rabbi finished peeling the last egg. "Rabbi smiled at the boys antics," Glinton (ibid.) reports, "and gave him four of the eggs without being asked." After dinner, Borin rushed home and told his father, who rushed over to B' Rabbi's house as soon as he heard the news. Rabbi "placed a plateful of eggs in front of Bouki," almost as soon as he arrived. Bouki gulped down the eggs and pressed Rabbi to tell him where he had gotten "all dese aig" (all these eggs) from. "In answer," Glinton (ibid., 133) tells us, "Rabbi smiled and promised to take Bouki to a farm where he could get more eggs than he could ever eat." The trap had been prepared. They agreed to meet at dawn the next morning.

Setting out very early the next day, Rabbi took Bouki and Borin to the farm, as promised, and showed them "the way into a barn where eggs were piled high in a heap of straw. Bouki went mad at the site of this treasure" (ibid.). Rabbi then outlined their plan of attack. While Borin and Bouki gathered the eggs, Rabbi suggested, he alone would go through the door that led into the next room and gather what he could there. Of course, the dim-witted Bouki, always vulnerable to reverse psychology, objected. He and Borin pushed past Rabbi and burst through the door. Rabbi's trap had sprung and so he ran away satisfied, imagining Bouki and Borin's fate. The barn door led to the farmer's bedroom and Bouki and Borin were duly punished for breaking and entering.

I recounted this narrative for two reasons. First, I believe it is representative of the hundreds of B' Bouki and B' Rabbi stories that are told and retold in the Bahamas. And, second, because I believe we can learn quite a bit about the values celebrated by Bahamians and about Bahamian beliefs and attitudes from a deeper look at this narrative. As Ogunleye (1997, 436) suggests, "Folklore contains seeds of wisdom, problem solving, and prophecy through tales of rebellion, triumph, reasoning, moralizing, and satire."

The Master Trickster, amongst other lessons, teaches that "cunning" is perhaps the most valuable tool in a person's arsenal; it's both a defensive and offensive weapon. If we are to believe the narrative, the world is full of people who will try to take advantage of you. Bouki and his son Borin, for instance, "tricked and cheated friend and foe alike" (ibid., 125). In such a world, a world where even your friends cannot be trusted, cunning is an important defense. Rabbi was able to recognize Borin's antics for what they were; he was not taken in by him. And, when pushed, he used his superior cunning to set a trap for Bouki and Borin.

It should also be noted that there was no proportionality to B' Rabbi's response; their pathetic efforts to trick a few free meals out of Rabbi is met with a sharp reprisal. While "cunning" is consistently applauded in these folk narratives, "low cunning" or an inability to be cunning is frequently disparaged; no fate is too harsh for the person who allows himself to get tricked.[16] Recall, Glinton (ibid., 125) described Bouki and Borin as "stupid, greedy and full of low cunning." Being full of low cunning appears last on the list of character flaws and for Bahamians it is the most damning. Remember, also, that being a "babe to the trade" of trickery was ultimately the cause of Borin's demise. It is perhaps not surprising that the same communities that applaud B' Rabbi because he is a master trickster, would fail to have any moral qualms about erecting fake lighthouses and luring unsuspecting ships to their ruin on the coral reefs.

Cunning is, thus, seen by Bahamians as a necessary tool for survival. As McFarlane (1998, 112) says of Anancy (B' Rabbi's Jamaican cousin),

> Anancy's ability to survive seemingly insurmountable odds, to outwit and confound the allegedly clever, and to disorient the strong and influential wins this unscrupulous creature much admiration. This West African folktale of the crafty spider has functioned as a pedagogical tool for teaching children survival skills. In spite of the fact that "it" is a confidence man, Anancy offers hope and relief to a disempowered population; persons who feel powerless can at least fantasize about using their weakness as a strength, albeit surreptitiously.

How did the Bahamas become the richest West Indian country although it is perhaps the poorest in terms of resources? Whether this response is accurate or not, the Bahamas' folk tradition would tell us that Bahamian entrepreneurs were more cunning, were better tricksters, than their counterparts in other contexts. Cunning is how the weak overcome (out-compete) the strong in Bahamian lore. Consider, for instance, the tale of *How Brer Rabby Tricked Brer Lion* adapted by Telcine Turner (1988).

B' Lion has fallen into a well and manages to convince B' Bouki (who just happened to be passing by) to help him to get out. The B' Bouki of Turner's tale (she calls him Brer Booky) is the same greedy figure that we met in Glinton's narrative and so it is not surprising that B' Bouki would be seduced by Brer Lion's promise to "reward him beyond his thinking." Salivating at his good fortune, B' Bouki rushed to get his "branch-and-vine" ladder and a relieved Brer Lion climbed it to safety. Instead of giving Bouki a reward, however, Brer Lion, as Turner (1988, 63) informs, "lurched toward him, growling. 'Now, I shall eat you!'" A surprised Bouki narrowly escapes Brer Lion's attack. "But I set you free," Bouki laments, "and you promised to reward me beyond thinking." Brer Lion's reply is both haunting and amusing; "eating you *would* be a reward beyond thinking" (ibid.). Brer Lion, however, feeling merciful, gives Bouki a chance; if B' Bouki can find the starving Brer Lion an alternate food source he will allow Bouki to live. With that they set out through the forest, Bouki leading the way looking for something or someone else to feed to Brer Lion.

On the way, they run into Brer Dog, Brer Frog and B' Rabbi (who she calls Brer Rabby). Brer Dog and Brer Frog's response to Bouki's plight are classically Bahamian. As I argued earlier, "low cunning" is an almost unpardonable quality in Bahamian (folklore) figures. Both Brer Dog and Brer Frog refuse to offer Bouki any advice or assistance. "I rescued Brer Lion from a deep hole. Do you think he should eat me?" Bouki queries them. Their replies are short and to the point; "I would," for instance, is all Brer Frog "croaks" in response. B' Rabbi, however, decides to use his wits to save his friend. "Your Supreme Majesty," Rabbi replies to the same question put to him by Bouki, "I am disappointed that you should consider dining on such a worthless creature" (Turner 1988, 64). And, then to B' Bouki he said, "You think I was born yesterday? That I would believe a scrawny, dull-witted goat like you could save anyone? You will have to prove it." Angered by Rabbi's insult, B' Bouki trudges back to the hole to prove his case.

On seeing the hole and the ladder, Rabbi became even more indignant. "You silly goat," Rabbi argued, "Do you think I would believe such a flimsy structure can bear the weight of His Majesty?" And, to Brer Lion, B' Rabbi offered, "Surely this lying good-for-nothing creature is unworthy of the regal appetite." This last insult pushes Bouki over the top and he lunges at Rabbi, blind with anger. Brer Lion, however, steps in between them. "After five days without food anything would be worth eating," Brer Lion asserted. "Still, to prove the truth of this goat's story and that he deserves to be my next meal," Brer Lion continues, "I shall demonstrate." With that, we learn from Turner (1988, 65), "Brer Lion climbed down the hole." As soon as he reached the bottom, B' Rabbi pulled up the ladder, trapping Brer Lion.

Cunning again proves the critical defense mechanism. Another theme that is clearly evident from this tale, however, is the notion that "unfettered greed" is not a virtue. Greed is hardly (if ever) portrayed as a good in Bahamian B' Bouki and B' Rabbi narratives. While *getting over*, that is, getting something for nothing or prevailing by your wiles rather than by your work, is often praised, greediness is seldom if ever glorified. In fact, it is denigrated almost as often as cunning is celebrated in these tales. We saw this clearly in Glinton's adaptation of *The Master Trickster.* Glinton (ibid., 128), for example, disparagingly called Bouki, "Bouki-of-the-Bottomless-Belly" who "ate what he was given and asked for more." And, it is Bouki and Borin's greed that stung B' Rabbi's sensibilities in *The Master Trickster.* Also, it is their greed that ultimately gets them into trouble. This theme reoccurs in *B' Rabby Makes B' Boukee his Cart Horse* where Rabbi tricks a greedy Bouki into serving as his pack horse. This theme also occurs in Glinton's (1993) adaptation of *The Sperrit House.*

Glinton begins her treatment by comparing the two friends. Rabbi we learn, for instance, "was so sharp, he could teach a wasp a better way to sting. He could smell the [odors] from a pot and tell whether the cook had added goat peppers or bird peppers. Being a thief, Bouki's friend could look at a field of ripened corn and estimate to the last grain how much he could steal without getting caught" (Glinton 19993, 59). Rabbi was truly a figure to admire. Bouki, however, "was different. On a good day, one and one could be three or four or, on a bad day as many as sixteen" (ibid., 60). And, while Rabbi was able to *control his passions* and was as *brave as a lion,* Bouki was both greedy and a coward. Turner captured the consequences of these differences quite succinctly in *The House in the Sky* (1988), her adaptation of the same tale. "Brer Booky," she tells us, "could hardly find food for his family. On the other hand, Brer Rabby's household looked plump and prosperous" (Turner 1988, 52). In spite of these differences, they were still friends, "united in their love of food and the desire to do as little as possible to get it" (Glinton 1993, 60).

One day, Rabbi mentions to Bouki that he knows a good place where they could find food and so the two set out on their quest the very next day at the crack of dawn. When they reached the appropriate spot, a clearing in the middle of the forest, Rabbi told his friend, who by now was quite confused, what was going on. Apparently, a couple of days before Rabbi had been in this same clearing when he heard someone singing a song and then saw a *sperrit (spirit) house* descend from the heavens to the ground. Rabbi of course (not one to miss an opportunity) had committed the song the *sperrit* sang to memory and so was able to sing it again on the day when he came with Bouki to search for easy plunder. As he sang it, the house came down as promised and the pair went inside. The door closed behind them and the house returned to the heavens. A mouth watering *sperrit feast* was prepared and laid out on the dinning room table; "juicy sides of beef, legs of mutton and huge hams, all roasted and ready to eat" (Glinton ibid., 64). Bouki, Glinton (ibid.) tells us, "ran here and there . . . grabbing handfuls of this, a bowlful of that, trying manfully to stuff a quart of food at a time into a mouth, which was made to hold no more than a half pint." Rabbi, on the other hand, "found an empty sack and carefully packed it with small portions of all the things he liked. He was neat about it, cutting and sampling in such a clever way that nobody but another Rabbi could tell that the dish had been disturbed." When he was finished packing his sac, B' Rabbi grabbed it up, sang the appropriate words (to bring the house out of the heavens) and left. Bouki, however, unable to tear himself away from this windfall, did not follow. Instead, he ate and danced to the point of exhaustion, collapsed, rolled under the bed and fell asleep.

When dusk came, the *sperrits* came home and realizing that someone had broken into their home began searching for the intruder. When they found Bouki under the "baby *sperrits*" bed, "the papa *sperrit* grabbed his kukumakai [magic] stick and poked at Bouki under the bed. Still drowsy, Bouki stumbled out to be greeted by a rain of blows" (Glinton 1993, 67). Though Bouki pleaded for his life, "the sperrit paid no heed to Bouki's pleas. He might have been beating him still, if the sperrit child had not taken pity on Bouki and sung the house down" (ibid.). Bouki escaped out of the house into the night.

Greed isn't always so good. Being greedy, the B' Bouki and B' Rabbi narratives teach us, is a costly habit. Surprisingly, the pirates who were headquartered in the Bahamas were more like Rabbi than Bouki in this regard. I am not suggesting that the pirates did not try to suck their victims dry. Cordingly (1995, 107) notes, for instance, that contrary to popular conceptions, a "common feature of the attacks was that the pirates took their time over looting the ships." But, the pirates did not attempt to grab all they could carry; they did not heedlessly attack every ship that seemed vulnerable. As Cordingly (ibid., 114) reports, the pirates often followed a ship for hours, sometimes days, in order to appraise their potential victims strengths and weaknesses. If it proved to be too powerful, "the pirates would veer away and seek a weaker victim." Also, the pirates were less about amassing treasure and more about enjoying the spoils of their conquests. An oft quoted section of Blackbeard's log, for instance, notes that his crew did not become restless until they had run out of rum. "Such a day," Blackbeard (cited in Lane 1998, 192) penned, "rum all out— our company somewhat sober— a damn'd confusion amongst us! Rogues a-plotting— great talk of separation— so I look'd sharp for a prize— such a day, took one, with a great deal of liquor on board, so kept the company hot, damned hot, then all things went well again."

The B' Rabbi that appears in *The Master Trickster, How Brer Rabby Tricked Brer Lion* and *The Sperrit House,* indeed the B' Rabbi of *B'Rabby makes B'Boukee his Cart Horse, Starvation, B'Rabby, B'Whale and B'Elephant* and the countless other B' Rabbi narratives (and versions of familiar B' Rabbi narratives) that float around the Bahamas, has a lot in common with the pirates who were once headquartered in the Bahamas. B' Rabbi and the Bahamian pirates were cunning, brave and sometimes ruthless.[17] With all the similarities between the mythical trickster and the real life Blackbeard, that is, with all the links that can be drawn between the B' Rabbi tales that dominate Bahamian folklore and the pirate narratives that appear in Bahamian history books it is not surprising that piracy would evolve as a metaphor for doing business in the Bahamas. Indeed, the pirate is explicitly celebrated in the Bahamas.

Lessons from their Pirate Past

As Craton and Saunders (1992, 113) contend, "elements of the piratical ethos remained embedded in the Bahamian consciousness." While the streets and taverns and caves and watchtowers named after Blackbeard (and his friends) may be more a part of the "brochure discourse" that Bahamians are forced to engage in to promote their tourist industry than some genuine statement of Bahamian culture,

> What is one to make of the naming of a line of Out Island mailboats after Major Stede Bonnet, the Barbadian desperado executed for piracy in South Carolina in 1718? More curious still, [is the existence] of the mysterious Abaconian folk figure of Old Bunce – half Guy Fawkes, half mummery monster – paraded through the streets of Green turtle Cay each New Year's Day to provoke amusement and exact tribute, who is seemingly, named after Phineas Bunce, one of the pirates executed by the first royal governor, Woodes Rogers, also in 1718. (Craton and Saunders 1992, 114)

And, although the *Pirates of Nassau* museum (for a time the only active museum in the Bahamas) can be dismissed as a mere tourist attraction, that it draws a great deal of Bahamian students and adults can not be as easily ignored. Also, *Pirates* on Bay Street (at least at the time of writing) was the nightclub of choice for young Bahamian professionals and returning college students.

Perhaps even more troubling, however, is that piracy is celebrated in the two contemporary, comprehensive, written histories of the Bahama Islands: Michael Craton's *A History of the Bahamas* and *The Story of The Bahamas* written by Paul Albury.[18] Everybody who has passed through a Bahamian junior high or high school in the last thirty or so years has been compelled to read and re-read both these books.[19] As such, their potential impact on Bahamian attitudes and culture, more broadly conceived, can not be exaggerated. The contents of these texts and the manner, that is, the style and tone with which the authors deal with their subjects are, therefore, critical for us to consider.

Albury's (1975) treatise, although not ostensibly an economic history, divides the Bahamian past according to its prevailing industries. The pirate years, the wrecking years and the decline in between are all given separate chapters; even though they lasted for variable lengths. Chapters have titles like *Privateers and Pirates, Boom and Bankruptcy, The Wrecking Industry* and *War and Whisky.* Craton's ([1962] 1986) chronicle, though not arranged in the same manner as Albury's, has a similar emphasis on the Bahamas' economic history.

Not only are the same phenomena emphasized but the manner in which they are dealt with are also quite similar. As suggested before, both books celebrate *pirate-like* industries and profane the less successful and more mundane economic activities that Bahamians have engaged in. Stated another way, both Albury and Craton celebrate *piracy* and, because of the prominence of their publications, promote the survival of *piracy as a metaphor for business* in the Bahamas. Indeed, the pirate as hero is a dominant theme in both of these books. As Albury (1975, 60) confesses,

> The swashbuckling nature of these daredevils calls forth an admiration tinged with envy. We admire their sheer courage, the valour with which they faced great odds, the defiance with which they fronted all the forces of law and order, and even death itself.

Craton ([1962] 1986, 90-91) exhibits a similar deference when describing Blackbeard, one of the most colorful pirates headquartered in the Bahamas,

> In the person of "Blackbeard" has been concentrated the whole disreputable spirit of his age. In the popular mind he is practically a synonym for Bahamian piracy.

> The sum total of the stories about Blackbeard is, of course, a caricature, though an instructive one. The Edward Teach of whom we read was villian of more than vile aspect. The hair of his beard he wore in plaits. Ranting into battle, he wore six brace of pistols in a special belt and fuming slow-matches in his hatband. In a cruel age, his cruelties were legendary. A physical giant, he is said to have had fourteen "wives" and when eventually cornered in 1718 to have gone on fighting after five musket wounds and three sabre-thrusts. His drinking powers were unmatched. One favourite story tells how, at the climax of a drunken spree, he forced his companions to enter the hold of a ship where he had set trays of burning sulphur. Closing the hatches, he shouted, "We have made our own hell. Let us see who is closest kin to the devil by staying longest in it!" One by one his spluttering cronies pushed up the hatches and grasped in the fresh air. Needless to say, the triumphant Blackbeard was last on deck, hardly the worse for his experience.

In Craton's hands, Blackbeard seems less a villain and more an heroic figure. His bravery is admired, his prowess as a pirate celebrated, his violent nature glorified and his person, because of his colorfulness, is beloved.

The way Albury and Craton have described the pirate-like industries that thrived in the Bahamas in different epochs are also worth recounting. When discussing the wrecking industry, Albury (1975, 140) writes,

> The stories that can be told about the wreckers would entertain an audience for forty days and forty nights. That there was a strong sense of fair play among them, and that wrecking permeated every strata of society is illustrated by the following incident. In a wrecking town, the morning church service had begun on a Sunday when from outside there rose the cry: 'Wreck ashore !' Immediately there was a movement toward the doors. The minister, with complete understanding of the situation, commanded: 'Keep your seats please. We will have one minute of prayer for the success of this voyage, and then we will all start fair.' After beseeching the blessings of the Lord, there was a hasty rush to the seashore and the wrecking vessels, with the minister in the lead.

And, when describing the extra-ordinary success of blockade running, Craton ([1962] 1986, 217) offers,

> Nassau has never known a more frenzied interlude before or since. Perhaps J.H. Stark did not exaggerate when he wrote in 1891 that "everyone was mad with excitement during these years of war. The shops were packed to ceilings, the streets were crowded with bales, boxes and barrels. Fortunes were made in a few weeks or months. Money was spent and scattered in a most extravagant and lavish manner. The town actually swarmed with Southern refugees, captains and crews of blockade-runners. Every available space in or out of doors was occupied. Men lay on verandahs, walls, decks and floors. Wages were doubled, liquor flowed freely and the common labourer had his champagne and rich food. Not since the days of the buccaneers and pirates had there been such times in the Bahamas; success paid larger premiums than were ever attained by any legitimate business in the world's commercial history."

Craton (with the aid of Stark) makes us nostalgic for that epoch. He makes us long for that excitement and that prosperity and, as a result, he supports the notion that only through *pirate-like* activities are either possible.

The esteem in which Albury and Craton hold their pirate subjects stands in sharp contrast with the contempt that they have for the more *legitimate* but less profitable agricultural and fishing industries that have flourished in the Bahamas at various periods. Craton's (ibid., 239) description of the sponging industry of the 1930s is telling,

> Although sponging was the backbone of the Bahamian economy for three-quarters of a century, no-one ever became very rich from the trade. Even if the total value of the sponge in the best years had been divided equally among the fishermen this would have produced the lordly average of £25 a head per year.
>
> The sponging voyages usually lasted from five to eight weeks. The value of the catch was almost wholly dependent upon the skill of the fishermen and the luck of the weather.
>
> On the voyage home the sponges were clipped, graded and strung in the rigging to dry. The stench of a homing sponger was unforgettable.

Sponging required Bahamians to work hard, tolerate difficult conditions and, in the end, offered them little reward.

Albury's disdain for the more mundane alternatives to piracy and smuggling and pessimism regarding their potential is less disguised than Craton's. Albury (ibid., 78), for instance, makes claims like "[they] were confronted with land more stubborn than any they had ever tried to work before. In fact nothing looked very promising." And,

> The resources of the land and the sea had been sufficient to feed the population but it had been difficult to stretch them beyond that. Companies and settlers had hoped for reasonable returns for their efforts but both had failed. There seemed to be no way to achieve success from the products of Bahamian sea and soil. When prosperity did come, it was generated by events far removed from Bahamian shores. (ibid., 85)

By "events far removed," Albury meant phenomena like the American Civil War which made blockade running profitable and Prohibition which spurred the development of a vibrant rum smuggling industry. Engaging in agriculture or fishing is considered hard, perhaps noble, but nonetheless fruitless and, in Albury's view, these efforts have not and will not be as successful as those piratical industries that thrived in the Bahamas. That Albury labeled the chapter that deals with the sisal, tomato and sponging industries that flourished in the 1930s, *Hard Times*, is further evidence that he holds this view.

Given these characterizations, it is easy to imagine a Bahamian student *reading* these histories as an indictment of agriculture and fishing and a celebration of piracy. Admittedly, this *read* is not the only one possible and the Albury and Craton books are not the only *texts* available to Bahamian businessmen and potential businessmen. Bahamians are able to draw on folklore, besides the B' Rabbi narratives, written histories besides Albury's and Craton's, literature, music and the visual arts. That other *readings* of Bahamian history are possible, however, does not prevent us from asserting that the pirate as hero is a dominant theme in Bahamian culture. Indeed, with piracy existing as a definite model of attaining wealth in the Bahamas and a metaphor for doing business, the *master pirate* has emerged as an ideal type of the Bahamian entrepreneur.

The Master Pirate: The Bahamian Entrepreneur as an Ideal Type

> The master pirate had to be able to handle his ship (in the beginning often an unseaworthy one until he could steal a better) in tempests and in fights, make his way disabled to sheltering harbours, control his unruly ruffians through disease and discontent, employ the arts of the diplomat to provide himself with a safe market on shore for his stolen wares. Men like these are rare, and few of the respectable professions can show more masterful personalities than those to be met at the top of the pirate tree.
>
> Gosse (1932, 2)

Remember that focusing on the ideal-typical, the quintessential entrepreneur in a particular culture is the appropriate way to examine the impact that culture has had on economic life in that context. As Mises ([1949] 1963, 59) explains, "Ideal types are specific notions employed in historical research and in the representation of its results. They are concepts of understanding." And, as Lavoie (1991, 36) has argued, "Entrepreneurship necessarily takes place within culture, it is utterly shaped by culture, and it fundamentally consists in interpreting and influencing culture." [20]

The *master pirate* is firmly rooted in the Bahamian context and has been profoundly affected by Bahamian culture. That throughout its history the Bahamas' economy has enjoyed short periods of extraordinary prosperity from piratical enterprises followed by prolonged periods of depression and decline has made Bahamian entrepreneurs particularly alert to *profiteering* opportunities, that is, opportunities to "get something for nothing" or to capture extraordinary rents through *piratical* activities. This alertness to *profiteering* rather than profit opportunities has meant that Bahamian entrepreneurs tend to have (i) narrow radiuses of trust and (ii) high time preferences.

Like the pirates who were headquartered in the Bahamas, the *master pirate* has a narrow radius of trust. Pirates and smugglers who were too open about their profiteering opportunities risked not only their profit but their freedom and, possibly, their lives. The B' Bouki and B' Rabbi tales that, as I have said, are by far the most prominent tales in Bahamian folklore also reinforce the low trust (trickster) culture that affects business dealings in the Bahamas.[21] Cunning, you may remember, is portrayed as our most critical asset and even our friends, we are taught, are out to trick us.

The omnipresent *master pirate* can also be accused of being impatient, that is, of having a short-term time horizon. Pirates in the Bahamas, indeed, pirates everywhere, were always at risk. At risk of going hungry because they let some ship, some profiteering opportunity, slip past. At risk of being preyed upon by their fellow pirates; honor amongst thieves could not really be counted on.[22] At risk of being captured and executed by any one of the colonial powers whose ships they threatened. As such, pirates did not (could not) see *piracy* as a long-term career nor did smugglers expect to be able to smuggle with impunity *ad infinitum*. As Albury (1975, 63) remarked, although "the pirates held undisputed sway in the Bahamas for about three years . . . whether there or elsewhere their careers were usually short lived. To quote Johnson, 'I must inform my readers that the far greater part of these rovers are cut short in the pursuit, by a sudden precipitation into the other world.'" Pirates, thus, focused primarily on satisfying their short term goals (current consumption tended to beat out long-term investments). As Lane (1998, 204) reports, "it was not uncommon for them to miss enormous payoffs due to drunkenness, infighting, or ignorance."

Although the *master pirate* has been an important (perhaps the most important) character in the economic life of the Bahamas, another ideal typical entrepreneur, albeit not as colorful as the master pirate, lives and operates in the Bahamas. The *enterprising slave*, like the *master pirate*, has had both historical success in the Bahamas and is a hero in Bahamian culture. Bahamians are not all or always opposed to hard work (even pirates worked hard) and a *spirit of enterprise* (as pronounced as it is anywhere) "infects" the Bahamian populace. In the next chapter, I explore the origins of the *enterprising slave* (even during slavery Bahamian blacks were peddlers) and tease out some of her major characteristics.

Notes

[1] It is important to note at this stage that mine is an effort to tell a cultural story; it is not an attempt at original historiography. Much more significant than the particulars of this or that aspect of Bahamian history is the meaning of that history, the way that Bahamians tell and understand that history, and the way that the Bahamas' economic story impacts the *web of meanings* that informs economic life in the Bahamas. To that end, I thought it best to take my cue from the way that others have told and understood this story. In many respects, the histories and stories commonly told in and about the Bahamas, their scope and tone, the episodes they choose to highlight and those they choose to downplay and not their subject matter are the "original source material" that bears most heavily on this effort.

[2] *The Pirates Own Book: Authentic Narratives of the Most Celebrated Sea Robbers* was published by the Marine Research Society in 1837. Volumes (almanacs) of that sort were very popular during that era and as that volume's editor remarks, "No other book preserves so extended an account of piracy, in ancient and modern times, in all parts of the world."

[3] As Defoe ([1724] 1972, 37) explains, "The Rovers being now pretty strong, they consulted together about getting some Place of Retreat, where they might lodge their Wealth, clean and repair their Ships, and make themselves a kind of Abode. They were not long in resolving, but fixed upon the Island of *Providence,* the most considerable of *Bahama Islands,* lying in the Latitude of about 24 Degrees North, and to the Eastward of the *Spanish Florida.* This Island is about 28 Miles long, and eleven where broadest, and has a Harbour big enough to hold 500 Sail of Ships; before which lyes a small Island, which makes two Inlets to the Harbour; at either Way there is a Bar, over which no Ship of 500 Tun can pass."

[4] As the Governor of Virginia wrote in 1717, "I doubt not Yor Lordps will use your Interest that sufficient Force be speedily dispatched to these Coasts for securing the Trade, and particularly to the Bahamas, to dislodge the Pyrates from thence, where they have settled their Generall Rendezvouse and seem to look upon these islands as their own" (cited in Craton 1986, 92).

[5] As Thompson (1979, 9) describes, "All wrecked goods were by law required to be brought to Nassau and sold at public auction at Vendue House. Since the Government regarded wrecked goods as regular imports, the Customs Authorities claimed a fifteen per cent duty on the goods sold at the time of sale before any other disbursements were made out of the sale proceeds."

[6] As Thompson (1979, 9) reports, "some 300 ships were licensed to engage in salvage in 1856 and some 2,679 Bahamians held individual wrecking licenses. In that year

wrecked goods were valued at £96, 304 and represented some 50 per cent of total imports."

[7] The same can be said about the drug trade. In the 1980s, the Bahamas served as a major transshipment point for illicit drugs headed for the United States from South America.

[8] The rum shipped from England and Scotland for illegal import into the United States was, ironically, subject to Bahamian custom's duties.

[9] Although profitable, these enterprises were, to use Baumol's (1990) phrasing, largely unproductive.

[10] The decline in exports after Prohibition was discontinued is illustrative. As Thompson (1979, 25) contends, "the repeal of the Eighteenth Amendment by the U.S. Congress in 1933 ended Prohibition and brought the rum-running business to an abrupt finish. In but a short time, the economy shifted from boom conditions to hard times." This theme of extraction instead of production also characterizes the relationship that Bahamian entrepreneurs have to the land. John Newman, a farmer on Long Island, describes the slash-and-burn techniques that were commonly practiced in the family islands. As he explains, "What we used to do before, what I used to do, I must say, we cut the bush ourselves. Let it dry and then burn it. Some people still do it here. [That way] you have more land cut down and you grow more fields" (Jenkins 2001, 121).

[11] In Storr (2002), *All We've Learnt: Colonial Lessons and Caribbean Underdevelopment,* I described how the belief that corruption, privilege and interventionism are the only avenues to attaining wealth has elevated these models of attaining wealth at the exclusion of others.

[12] The tragedy of the commons is a well documented phenomenon in economic literature and so will not be rehearsed here. Instead of focusing on that, what I will remind you of is the link between extractive industries and piracy. As I intimated earlier, it is important to recognize that neither these industries that attempt to exploit natural resources nor piracy are productive (in any real sense). Both are parasitic at their cores.

[13] As the Colonial Secretary reported in 1930, "The main obstacle to modern forms of cultivation in The Bahamas is probably to be found in the uncompromising character of the land which, at first sight, seems utterly impossible for cultivation and which in its natural state cannot give a high return per acre . . . Any attempt to develop agriculture to an advanced stage on this sort of land, . . . one is even surprised that anything can be extracted from what appears to be more or less barren rock" (Eneas 1998, 68).

[14] Oruç and Hayreddin were perhaps the two most infamous of the Barbary pirates. As Lane (1998, 11) describes, "Known to Europeans as Barbarossa (Italian for 'red-beard'), Oruç was followed in the pirate trade by his similarly red-bearded brother,

Hayreddin, in 1518, and these Barbary corsairs, the Barbarossa brothers, soon became legendary figures."

[15] As Craton and Saunders (1992, 109) describes, "Pirates were almost invariably volunteers, recruited from the ranks of ordinary seamen on naval or merchant ships, a brutalized and oppressed class which was itself the scourings of a landborne underclass. They were therefore motivated as much by a rejection of class oppression and by instincts of revenge as by a quest to escape from socioeconomic degradation through instant, if ill-gotten wealth . . . pirate captains were elected and ruled by consensus. They could be deposed, even executed, by their crews without taint of mutiny, and they enjoyed very few extra privileges – seldom even a separate cabin, dining table, or bed. Pirate crews met in common council to draw up their initial articles fixing duties and shares, to decide strategy and tactics, to settle disputes, or to determine the fate of captives or of crewmen breaking the pirate code of conduct."

[16] Indeed, "fool me once shame on you, fool me twice shame on me" is a familiar (oft repeated) refrain in Bahamian households.

[17] And, although it is true that the trickster/pirate has prospered in the Bahamas, this orientation to business life is not without its limitations (some quite severe). As MacFarlane (1998, 113) said of Anancy (B' Rabbi's cousin), "the problem with the Anancy culture is that its only consistency is its inconsistency; it is a moving target and consistently unreliable."

[18] Actually, a third one has recently come onto the scene. Craton, along with Gail Saunders, has penned *Islanders in the Stream: A History of Bahamian People*. This two-volume history, however, is still quite expensive and has not yet made its way into the Bahamian consciousness.

[19] Admittedly, that they were compelled to read and re-read these books says little about how they were received. The Russians under Stalin, for instance, were compelled to read Engels and Marx. Even still, many of them hated and rejected Marxism. To be sure, "a single text might take on a variety of meanings as different groups of people holding different positions in the social structure (as determined by socio-economic class, in particular) interpret the text from their particular perspective" (Lavoie and Chamlee-Wright 2000, 89). "In framing the way in which the story gets told," however, "the author constructs some of the 'limits and parameters' of the possible interpretations that the reader might take away" (ibid., 90). As such, the messages contained in these histories of the Bahamas can never be completely resisted and the way enterprise is viewed in Bahamian culture is necessarily affected by them. As Lavoie and Chamlee-Wright (2000, 93) suggest, "all viewers [and readers] play the messages they receive . . . against their own perspective, thereby reinforcing or challenging previously held assumptions and beliefs." Moreover, since many readers (in this instance) are not in a position to access the validity of the claims presented (most encounter these texts as teenagers) they may be particularly susceptible.

[20] Remember that entrepreneurship, as discussed here, is conceived broadly. In my view, it is as *legitimate* to talk about entrepreneurial stealing, vote selling and bribe taking as it is to talk about entrepreneurial arbitraging. There is an entrepreneurial element "present in all human action" and that element is an "alertness to possibly newly worthwhile goals and to possibly newly available resources" (Kirzner 1973, 31-35). Note, also, that these newly perceived means and ends are evaluated and selected subjectively. That is, individuals rooted in particular cultures and operating in particular contexts decide which goals are worthwhile and which ends they think will be effective.

[21] As MacFarlane (1998, 113) has said of Anancy, "The problem with the Anancy culture is that . . . it contradicts its own ethical aspirations. Since its ethic is one of survival, Anancy has no resolute moral standard but is characterized by deceit, dishonesty, double-talk, and back stabbing. Self-preservation becomes the driving force in all Anancy's social engagements. Truth is relative and situational, and trust is either an expendable commodity or a great liability."

[22] Indeed, many pirates (the famed Henry Morgan, Captain Kidd, etc.) became pirate hunters. See, for instance, Zacks (2002).

Chapter Four

Sankofa: The Spirit of Enterprise, The Legacy of a Peculiar Slavery

Introduction

The Bahamas is separated from the rest of the Caribbean islands by much more than a few miles of sea. Its economy, for instance, has simply had no rival in the region. Even though the Bahamas is poor, in terms of resources, saves less per capita and has a legal, regulatory and tax structure that looks very much like the analogous structures in Jamaica, Barbados and Trinidad, GDP per capita in the Bahamas is almost twice as high as it is in the next richest country in the West Indies.[1] The distance between the Bahamas and the rest of the Caribbean is also exaggerated by its disparate history: piracy and its correlates (as we have seen) play a much more pivotal role in the story of the Bahamas. And, much about the institution of slavery in the Bahamas was peculiar.

While 17th century piracy is an important chapter in the history of every Caribbean country, in the Bahamas piracy evolved as a dominant model for attaining economic success and a primary metaphor for doing business. Many of the successful industries in the Bahamas (piracy, wrecking, gun smuggling, and rum running) were piratical in nature. And, at various times in the Bahamas' economic narrative, the *master pirate* has been the principal figure in the plot (the driving force of the economy and the primary agent of change in the tale).

Slavery as it existed in the Bahamas, similar to piracy in that nation of islands, was also a "peculiar" institution. This is true even though the crack of the whip was just as loud, the sound of cold metal on warm black skins just as chilling and the stench of ships packed with human cargo just as strong in the Bahamas as it was in St. Lucia, Martinique and Aruba. Nuclear families were remarkably stable, however, amongst Bahamian slaves and slaves in the Bahamas were much healthier than slaves in Barbados, Trinidad, Jamaica, Haiti or Cuba. Similarly, Bahamian slaves seem to have had more "free" time, enjoyed much more autonomy (they could contract out their own labor) and attained a higher standard of living than their Caribbean cousins. And, as Johnson (2000, 47) asserts, "slaves in the Bahamas were more successful in retaining their culture than their American counterparts, and this was generally the case throughout the British West Indies." That *slavery everywhere was bad,* however, should not blind us to these differences; particularly, since there is much to be gained by differentiating the practice of slavery in the Bahamas from its practice elsewhere in the region. Indeed, it is my conjecture that by concentrating on the salient characteristics of the institution of slavery in the Bahamas we might learn something about the legacy of slavery in the Bahamas (and possibly in the wider Caribbean). Stated another way, by focusing on the peculiarities of Bahamian slavery, we will, I contend, gain some insight into how the *enterprising slave* evolved as a dominant figure in the Bahamas' economic story.

Five Days Slave and Two Days Peasant

> There was nothing quite like black slavery, in scale, importance or consequence. No other slave system was so regulated and determined by the question of race. No other slave system forcibly removed so many people and scattered them across such vast distances – and for such wonderful returns to the slave-owning class. Black slavery in the Americas, though it differed from one place to another, was unique. Looking back, it also seems bizarre. Here was a labour system called into being by

> Europeans, to develop their settlements in the Americas, using labour from Africa, and all to sate the palates of Europeans.
>
> Walvin (1992, ix)

By as early as 1667, King Sugar had been securely enthroned in the islands of the Caribbean (Williams 1970, 112). And, King Sugar, to be sure, was a tyrant. While promising slavers and plantation owners and overseers unparalleled riches, he condemned millions of Africans (and their descendents) to a frightful journey across the Atlantic ocean followed by a lifetime, if they survived the *middle passage*, of back-breaking toil. As Dunn (1972, 189) remarked, "the story of sugar was not all sweetness." Of the four million Africans who made the horrible "pilgrimage" to the *New World*, almost half of them, mercifully, died either during the trip or within a few years of their reaching the Caribbean. As Williams (1970, 147) reports, "For every 56 Negroes [alive] on the plantations at the end of three years, 44 had perished."

Those who survived were forced to do the work of horses and oxen; in the Caribbean "the plough was eschewed, and the man with the hoe" came to dominate the landscape (ibid., 113). King Sugar demanded human "beasts of burden" and his "happy helpers" (slavers and slave owners) happily provided him with millions of Africans for his edification. Within only a few years of King Sugar's coronation, the majority of West Indians were Africans in shackles. And, as Mintz and Hall (1970) have noted, not least amongst the myriad of social, economic and political dilemmas created by this "bizarre" social configuration was the problem of how to feed a group of people considered chattel and not empowered to feed and fend for themselves. As Mintz and Hall (ibid., 3) suggests,

> The alternative extremes were either to use the slaves to produce as much as possible of their own diet, by compulsion or by incentive, or else to import all of what they ate. Of these two courses the first . . . was ideally the more desirable. If the slaves could feed themselves the estates would be saved expenditure of money on imported foods and avoid the risks contingent upon importation.

In lieu of rations, estate owners and managers gave their slaves use-rights to the less arable plots on their plantations and "free-days" on Saturdays to facilitate them growing their own provisions. As such, the typical Afro-Caribbean in the 17th and 18th centuries was a slave five days out of every week and lived the life of a peasant planter on Saturday and Sunday.

In Lieu of Rations: Free Saturdays and Provision Plots

This practice, of offering slaves use-rights to provision "pens" and free Saturdays to man them in lieu of rations, seems to have accompanied the spread of sugar throughout the region. As Tomich ([1990] 1991, 306), informs us, "the diffusion of sugar cane entailed not merely the movement of a commodity but the spread of a whole way of life . . . Masters no longer distributed rations to their slaves. Instead, the latter were expected to provide their own food, shelter, clothing, and other material needs from the labor of their 'free' day." Although this "way of life" went against the *de jure* laws governing slavery in many of the Caribbean islands when it first emerged,[2] it nonetheless became a *de facto* norm in the region.[3]

"On every slave plantation," Sherlock and Bennett (1998, 164) report, "there was a portion of land called 'Negro grounds', out of which each slave was allotted a portion to cultivate." As Mathew Lewis ([1834] 1999, 54), the owner of Cornwall plantation in Jamaica, recounts in his journal, "although their cottages are always surrounded with trees and shrubs, their provision grounds are kept quite distinct, and are at a distance in among the mountains." The size of these "Negro grounds" varied considerably. Typically, however, they were each at least one hundred square feet. Couples dwelling together, reportedly, worked joint plots and households with children could petition for more land if they desired. As Lewis (ibid.) recounts, "all slaves maintain themselves in this manner by their own labour; even domestic attendants are not exempted, but are expected to feed themselves, except stated allowances of salt fish, salt pork, etc."

Virtually all the evidence from that period suggests that slaves met the challenge of fending for themselves enthusiastically. And, as such, took full advantage of this opportunity to carve out a "niche of freedom" within an exceedingly illiberal social order. As Klein (1986, 176) asserts, "these *conucos*, gardens or provisioning grounds, became the basis for an alternative peasant life style." Provision grounds were usually well tended and once slaves were given the autonomy and the authority to plant and tend to their own crops as they desired, the variety and quality of the produce they produced was nothing short of impressive. As Lewis ([1834] 1999, 68) recalls, "the provision-grounds of the negroes furnish them with plantains, bananas, cocoa-nuts, and yams; of the latter there is a regular harvest once a year, and they remain in great perfection for many months, provided they are dug up carefully . . . these vegetables form the basis of negro sustenance." Tomich ([1990] 1991, 312), in his discussion of "negro grounds" in Martnique, is similarly impressed by the variety of vegetables that the slaves cultivated. As he (ibid.) asserts, "Manioc, the principle source of nourishment of the slave population, was harvested as often as four times a year. Besides manioc, the slaves raised bananas, potatoes, yams, and other vegetables on these provision grounds." Reportedly, slaves in Martinique also grew sorrel, squash, green peppers, hot peppers, calabash vines, okra and tobacco on the "small gardens in the yards surrounding the slave cabins" (ibid.).

It is important to note that the use of provision grounds was not only a means of subsistence for the slaves but became a vital (and perhaps the only) space for "collective self-expression." As Tomich (ibid.) reports,

> The use of these parcels and their product was not simply a narrow economic activity but was integrated into broader cultural patterns. The work of preparing the soil, planting, cultivating, harvesting, and the disposition of the product were organized through ritual, kinship, and community and were important aspects of slave life as diverse as kinship, cuisine, and healing practices.

Indeed, Sherlock and Bennett (1998, 170) have argued that provision grounds and free Saturdays allowed nothing short of the recreation of Africa in the West Indies. Slaves fully exploited the autonomy they were granted; not only growing crops but developing and retaining Afro-Caribbean culture.

These provision plots (and the subsequent market activities that *slaves qua peasants* engaged in) were also critical spheres for slave resistance. As Beckles (1990, 59) recounts, "Resistance also took place in the economic area of the social order. Blacks had brought with them from West Africa a strong inclination for marketing, and sought to establish their own commercial patterns." Hall (1991, 343) concurs with this assessment, arguing that,

> In the last hundred years or so of slavery in the Danish Virgin Islands, the slaves by the use of the discretionary time, legally and illegally at their disposal, had created certain modes of being and behaviour that were distinctly theirs. The use of 'free' time was far more conducive to this purpose, having regard to the demanding nature of the routines and discipline associated with plantation production. By emancipation they had created a culture, neither wholly African nor yet European, retaining, adapting, borrowing and adopting.

Taking advantage of "free Saturdays and provision grounds," therefore, radically improved the slave's life and, not surprisingly, became an important part of his/her existence.

Consequently, slaves approached their regular chores differently than they did their work on their "own" grounds. Lewis' ([1834] 1999, 55) claim that their frequent visits to their provision grounds allows them "to perform their task with so much ease as almost converts it into an amusement," in this regard, is not entirely farfetched. Similarly, his claim that their frequent visits to "their grounds makes them grow habitually as much attached to them as they are to their houses and gardens" also seems accurate. As Klein (1986, 177) asserts, "That these gardens became a fundamental part of the slave life was indicated in every protest movement led by slaves in the 19th century. As the slave system began to break up, one of the first demands of the slaves was for more time on their own plots and the use of more lands for their gardens."

This "niche of freedom," however, should be kept in perspective. The *de facto* rights that the slaves enjoyed under this "free Saturdays and provision grounds in lieu of rations" practice were extremely tenuous. Blacks at this time, whether free or slave, had no standing in court and it should not be forgotten that enslaved Africans were considered property not persons. In fact, the 1688 *Slave Act* in Barbados "declared slaves as 'real estate' as opposed to mere chattel" (Beckles 1990, 34).[4] As Schoelcher (Tomich [1990] 1991, 311) informs, in such an environment, "the greater or lesser wealth of the slaves depends a great deal on the benevolence of the master." Or rather, it depended on slave owners recognizing that any additional perdition on their part would have had a deleterious effect on the slave's incentive to work his/her "pen." Because, "at times, the planters deprived them of their free day under various pretexts" (ibid., 312), however, slaves could never fully trust the practice.

Additionally, as stated earlier, provision grounds were usually situated on the least arable land. In Barbados, for instance, we know that "by 1670, all the colony's good arable land was under sugar cultivation" (Beckles 1990, 22). And, that in Jamaica, slaves had to grow their crops "in the mountains" (Lewis [1834] 1999, 54). Although some planters saw the allocation of provision lands as an opportunity for crop rotation, more often than not, slaves were allocated land that could not sustain commercial crops. Consequently, even the most industrious slaves faced a tough go. Tomich ([1990] 1991, 312), describing the situation in Martinique, notes that "they were generally given land that was incapable of supporting sugar or coffee." And, as Mintz and Hall (1970, 3) argue, "it is no accident that [even] today in the British Caribbean the peasantry and food production are found chiefly in mountain areas or in areas otherwise, by reason of location, or of soil or weather conditions, unsuitable for sugar production."

These constraints aside, the importance of these "pens" to both the material and psychological survival of Caribbean slaves can not be overstated. They became one of "the only places . . . [in the Caribbean] . . . where Africans were free to make their own decisions" (Sherlock and Bennett 1998, 170).[5] Unfortunately, we can only imagine how they might have thrived had their opportunities not been so constrained, that is, had they not been considered real estate and were, instead, allowed to participate fully in the economic life of their islands. Even with their shackles on, however, they managed to develop dynamic, thriving markets for their produce and products.

Everyone a Higgler: More Peasant than Chattel

The streets of Jamaica, of Haiti, of even Communist Cuba are always littered with higglers and hawkers. Little black angels disguised as children and stationed on every downtown street corner, proselytize with arms full of guineps, pears and plums. Women, beautiful like all grandmothers are beautiful, sitting on overturned Border's milk crates, offer to braid hair; "a dollar a plait." Dusty barefoot men with a cocunut in one hand and a cutlass in the other tempt you with "sweet water." Rastas on bicycles too small for their frames and a sack full of roasted peanuts announce their presence with a bellow: "peanuts! irie nuts! peanuts!" Pick-up trucks are converted to fish markets; this morning's catch of conch and crayfish and codfish and snappers spread out for their would-be suitors. Entrepreneurs, camped outside the food store with buckets full of crabs and baskets full of sugarcane and bananas, supply those items you won't find in doors. Everyday, except Sunday, is market day and the sounds, sights and smells of brown and black West Indians (the descendents of enslaved Africans) engaged in commerce, color the already vibrant landscapes of these island paradises. Indeed, the picture painted by their *spirit of enterprise* is remarkable. Even more remarkable is that the roots of these internal marketing systems reach back to pre-colonial/pre-slavery Africa and that brown and black West Indians managed to express their *enterprising spirits* even during the years they were in bondage.

"By the mid-eighteenth century the Sunday markets were popular economic institutions" (Beckles 1990, 60).[6] Monday through Friday field slaves were doing the back-breaking work of cultivating sugar cane. Evenings and Saturdays were spent in their own gardens, tending to their crops. And, since slaves produced a marketable surplus on their provision grounds, in addition to meeting their own subsistence needs, the desire/need to trade and barter their wares went hand in hand with the practice of "free Saturdays and provision plots." Sunday was a day on which, at least, field slaves traditionally had no duties and so it became a natural day on which to hold these desired markets.[7]

Slaves, reportedly, benefited quite a bit from this weekly opportunity to sell their produce and to shop for goods. They were able to both diversify their consumption baskets and take advantage of the gains to be had from specialization.[8] Some slaves, it seems, even became quite "well-off" as a result of their market activities. Slaves in Martinique, for instance, could earn as much as 700 francs a year (Tomich [1990] 1991, 316) and the most prosperous were able to furnish their homes "elaborately" with "chairs, tables, chests of drawers, mirror wadrobes and even four-poster beds with pillows, sheets and mattresses" (ibid., 315). As slave owner Matthew Lewis ([1834] 1999, 71; *emphasis added*) recounts, "besides the profits arising from their *superabundance* of provisions, which the better sort of negroes are enabled to sell regularly once a week at Savannah la Mar to a *considerable* amount, they keep a *large stock* of poultry, and pigs *without number*." Although words like "superabundance" are undoubtedly overstated, that slaves could improve their quality of life by selling "regularly once a week" should not be doubted. To be sure, Mintz and Hall (1970, 16) report that by 1774, according to one estimate, over 20% of the currency circulating the island of Jamaica was held by slaves.

These markets, however, were not only important to the slaves who participated in them but became central to the economies where they operated. In Barbados, for instance, "slave hucksters" competed with "white small farmers" (Beckles 1990, 60) and in Jamaica they supplied everything from fruits and vegetables to pigs and goats. As Mintz and Hall (1970, 16) report, "by [1774], the slaves were not only central to the economy as the producers of the cash export commodities, principally sugar, but had also become the most important suppliers of foodstuffs and utilitarian craft items to all Jamaicans."

Because these *slave qua entrepreneur* dominated internal markets became so central to the maintenance of the *slave qua chattel laborer* dominated economies in the West Indies, they were at the same time quite extraordinary and deeply contradictory (Sherlock and Bennett 1998). By exploiting the practice of free Saturdays and market Sundays, by being industrious and enterprising, enslaved Africans were giving "legs" to a system designed to confine and control them. It is, indeed, ironic that while enslaved, West Indians not only *retained* but further *developed* the skills and the *spirit of enterprise* that are so vital to economic development. Tomich ([1990] 1991, 315) is right when he argues that,

> The markets offered incentives to the slaves and enabled them to improve the material conditions of life as well as to acquire skills, knowledge, and social contacts that increased their independence and allowed them to assert their individuality and vary the texture of their lives. Their initiative led to the development of new economic and social patterns and the mobilization of productive forces that otherwise would have remained dormant.

That West Indians have not managed to translate these *awakened skills* into riches, however, remains a nagging problem. Still, it is impossible to discount the impact that this spirit of enterprise has had on the lives of West Indians; affecting both the way they do business and the way they perceive of their opportunities for success. The proto-peasantry that evolved throughout the Caribbean during slavery continues to be an important force in West Indian economic life. Nowhere has this class of peasants thrived more than in the Bahamas

> I felt strongly tempted to set him at liberty at once; but if I were to begin in that way, there would be no stopping; and it would be doing a kindness to an individual at the expense of all my other negroes – others would expect the same; and then I must either contrive to cultivate my estate with fewer hands – or must cease to cultivate it altogether – and, from inability to maintain them, *send my negroes to seek bread for themselves – which, as two thirds of them have been born upon the estate,* and many of them are lame, dropsical, and of a great age, *would, of all misfortunes that could happen to them, be the most cruel.*
>
> Lewis ([1834] 1999, 51; *emphasis added*)

It is my contention that Lewis (ibid.) could not have been more mistaken. Rather than being the cruelest "of all misfortunes that could happen to them," it would not only have improved their lives markedly but possibly also improved the lives of their progeny. Indeed, it is my conjecture that one of the reasons that Bahamians have prospered is because they, even when they were slaves, and their descendants, who were born free, were forced to "to seek bread for themselves." Slavery in the Bahamas differed from slavery elsewhere in the region in two significant ways: Bahamian slaves (a) were allowed to self-hire and (b) had more free time to devote to their provision grounds and market activities. It is to these differences that I now turn my attention.

More Capitalist than Capital

The most industrious slaves in the Bahamas, like their enterprising cousins throughout the region, were never fully dependent on rations. Indeed, because "as much land was set aside for the use of the slaves as was needed for their provisions," they were able to maintain themselves (Craton and Saunders 1992, 299).[9] Bahamian slaves were "free" to work their own grounds whenever they did not have official tasks to perform and were generally "expected" to work them on their "free" Saturday afternoons. Typically,

> Half an acre was allotted as a garden for each house, 'as the property of the occupant for the time being,' with further pasturage for hogs and fowls. Keeping the number of small stock under control was obviously a problem. Each family head was allowed one breeding sow, as long as it was kept in a pen, but for those who had one, a quart of corn was stopped from the slaves' weekly allowance, to be fed to the free-running hogs. Further to prevent overgrazing, all these hogs were to be sold as soon as they were 'fit for the spit,' with the exception of one that might be kept in a pen for slaves' consumption. The owner had the right of pre-emption of all hogs, poultry, and eggs but agreed to pay . . . market prices, as fixed by the driver and two persons chosen by the seller.
>
> (Craton and Saunders 1992, 299)

Bahamian slaves like their Caribbean cousins enjoyed *de facto* use-rights over some portion of their owner's estate and could dispose of their produce as they liked (see Saunders 1985, 158-159). Not surprisingly, markets for surplus provisions developed in settlements throughout the archipelago. Bahamian slaves like slaves in Jamaica, Barbados and Trinidad, "could [then] get permission to attend market[s] in town . . . as long as their grounds were in good order, they had provisions to sell, and the weather was not inclement" (Craton and Saunders 1992, 299).[10]

These provision grounds and markets became ever more important to the welfare of slaves in the Bahamas and, on their strength, Bahamian slaves attained far better health and demographic statistics than slaves in the sugar colonies. Bahamian slaves, for instance, tended "toward monogamous marriages and the maintenance of stable nuclear families" to a greater degree than slaves elsewhere (ibid., 295).[11] And, as Craton and Saunders (ibid., 310) inform us, Bahamian slaves had a better than average diet, lower morbidity and mortality rates and higher rates of fertility than slaves in other Caribbean countries. What should we make of these demographic patterns? It is my conjecture that understanding the nature and failure of the Bahamian plantation system is the key to understanding these demographics.

Recall that the plantation economy never really got off the ground in the Bahamas. Its first few years, however, were quite promising. "For the first few years after the crops began to come in," Albury (1975, 115) reminds us, "planters were handsomely rewarded for their industry." Cotton, to be sure, "became a sort of 'white-gold' which dominated all Bahamian economic thinking" and thousands of Africans were brought in to do the "mining" (ibid.). Unfortunately, for the plantation owners, the Bahamian pests and the Bahamian soils did not cooperate with their efforts. The chenille worm destroyed most of the 1789 crop and it, along with the red bug which stained and so ruined fibers, plagued farmers for the next few years.

As stated before, however, the Bahamian soil was the real *spoiler*. As McKinnen wrote, "although nature in all of . . . (the islands) . . . spontaneously brings forth many vegetables both curious and beautiful, she has hitherto refused to resign herself to continued cultivation" (Albury 1975, 116). Bahamian soils are "thin, scattered, and easily exhausted" and were, thus, never suited for the production of either cotton (the commercial crop they tried to cultivate) or sugar (Craton and Saunders 1992, 196). "Besides, the clearing of the natural cover for making cotton fields, coupled with the occasional heavy rains, speeded erosion and the leaching of what soils there were" (ibid.).

When the plantation system inevitably collapsed, Bahamian slaves ended up with a great deal of time to devote to their subsistence and market activities. And, as a result, they were able to both improve their standard of living and develop the skills and practices necessary to maintain a market economy. As Craton and Saunders (ibid., 310) remarked,

> The effectiveness of a slave's diet, of course, related mainly to the type and amount of work required, with most Bahamian slaves benefiting from the converse of that inexorable equation that said that the more work demanded by the master the more food was needed by the slave yet the less time was available to grow it. The steady decline of the plantation economy thus meant, in general, the steady improvement in the slaves' diet, and consequently in the statistics of health and demographic performance.

As the soils in the Bahamas eroded, those planters who did not abandon their plantations found themselves forced to give their slaves more time to grow provisions. They simply could not afford to give their slaves rations given the meager and (sometimes) nonexistent profits they were earning from their farms. As Craton and Saunders (ibid., 314) summarize, "not only was the improving demographic health of the Bahamian slaves related to the declining plantation economy, but to the average planter's declining expectation of profit for his estate [which] was coupled [to] the slaves' rising expectation of being left on their own."[12]

That it was cotton rather than sugar that Bahamian planters attempted to grow also had a marked difference on the quality of life that Bahamian slaves enjoyed. As Craton and Saunders (ibid., 310) inform us,

> Cotton cultivation and harvesting could [n]ever compare with the almost year-round gang labor of sugar production – especially the backbreaking toil of cane holing in stiff clays, or cutting and carrying the cane to the pitiless tempo of the mill. Cotton bushes are planted as seeds and grow easily in lightly hoed land. Plucking and cleaning the cotton bolls are tedious tasks, but not desperately strenuous, and the pace of the crop is not driven by either a short flowering season or a tendency of the product to decay as soon as picked.

Although the poor soil in the Bahamas meant that cotton production in the Bahamas was still quite hard work, it could not compare to the production of sugar. And, Bahamian slaves were, as a result, better situated to exploit their free time than slaves elsewhere.

Cotton cultivation also meant that slaves were employed mostly by the task system; slaves on sugar plantations usually worked in gangs. Under the task system, slaves were assigned either a particular chore to perform or were made responsible (or partially responsible) for cultivating a specific section of the plantation.[13] As McKinnen (cited in Cash, et al, 1991, 192) describes,

> Their labor is allotted to them daily and individually, according to their strength; and if they are so diligent as to have finished it at an early hour,

> the rest of the day is allowed to them for amusement or their private concerns. The master also frequently superintends them himself; and therefore it rarely happens that they are so much subject to the discipline of the whip as where the gangs are large, and directed by agents or overseers.

Bahamian slaves, thus, benefited from the task system in several significant respects. First, they were not "so much subject to the discipline of the whip as where the gangs are large." Also, slaves under the task system gained valuable lessons in the benefits of the division of labor and specialization. Finally, the task system made slaves, at least in part, residual claimants; they were held accountable for fulfilling their tasks and benefited "if they [were] so diligent as to have finished it at an early hour."

It is my conjecture, however, that the "lessons" Bahamian slaves learnt under the task system and the greater autonomy that Bahamian slaves enjoyed because of the decline of the plantation system not only resulted in their being able to achieve a higher standard of living than slaves in other Caribbean colonies but, at least in part, explains the unusual "yen and flair" that attends even small scale ventures in the Bahamas. Although provision plots and slave-run markets became important in other colonies, slaves elsewhere still spent the bulk of their time engaged in production for which they received no compensation. The predominance of this unnatural relationship in these contexts not only capped their earning potential (the more time they spent working the plantation the less time they could spend in the market and on their provision grounds) but curtailed their dreams. Bahamians, however, came to view the higgler traditions as more than a means of subsistence but as an opportunity to attain real economic success.

Growing one's business was and continues to be seen as a real opportunity in the Bahamas. Bahamians expect a better than subsistence life (or at least believe that one is possible). Glinton-Meicholas (1994, 64; *emphasis added*), Bahamian social critic, has noticed the same sentiments. "Bahamians have," she suggests, "an extraordinary yen and flair for entrepreneurship and all the necessary optimism. Our people will open little shops or roadside stalls with little more than a hope, a prayer and price list." Bahamians actually believe, she continues, that "a permanent location is not a requirement for launching a *highly profitable* business in The Bahamas."

Indeed, in Jamaica, Martinique and Cuba, slaves became acutely aware that a *culture of privilege* existed and that, no matter what their efforts were, no more than marginal improvements to their quality of life could be had (see Storr 2002). For slaves in the Bahamas, however, the barriers to their economic success, to their attaining a higher living standard, however, were not so indelibly etched.[14] That many Bahamians descend from the large population of free blacks that settled in the Bahamas only lessens the deleterious lessons (of inferiority and inadequacy) taught by slavery.[15] Bahamians, therefore, recognized before their Caribbean cousins that they had the potential to be more than higglers and that their labor could result in more than subsistence. That Bahamian slaves were often allowed to hire themselves out speaks to both the distinctiveness of Bahamian slavery and the potential of Bahamian slaves to earn a "decent" living.

The "Peculiarity" of Self-Hire

Johnson (1996) in his important contribution to Bahamian socio-economic history, *The Bahamas From Slavery to Servitude*, offers us a detailed description of the self-hire system that evolved in New Providence. "Unlike most of the other British Caribbean colonies of this period," Johnson (ibid., 33) informs us, "the Bahamas produced none of the labor-intensive tropical staples that required a closely supervised workforce and kept the slaves steadily employed." As a result, slave owners found it difficult to find productive activities for their slaves. Many *masters* faced with this dilemma, simply, "allowed their slaves to seek their own employment in return for a sum, mutually agreed upon, that was paid to them at regular intervals . By that arrangement, labor services that were due to the slave owners were commuted into cash payments" (ibid., 34).[16]

Both parties benefited from this relationship. Masters enjoyed a steady stream of income from their slaves; an occurrence that would have otherwise been atypical in the Bahamas because of its poor soil. And, slaves were able to, in a sense, buy themselves a little window of freedom. So long as they paid their "wages" (ironically the name given to the fee they had to pay their masters in order to be allowed to seek work) they were left alone, outside the surveillance and direct control of their owners. Slaves under the self-hire system were allowed to not only search for employers but to negotiate their salaries. As Johnson (ibid., 36) informs us, "by the late 1790s, slaves on self-hire controlled important areas of the urban economy." And, "In 1799, for example, [there were complaints] that slave middlemen were monopolizing the supply of fruits, ground provisions, and vegetables in Nassau and forcing up prices" (ibid.). Similarly, "slaves on self-hire were successfully dictating wage levels in their negotiations with employers." (ibid.). By 1800, the slaves on the self-hire system were demanding and earning wages that were not only high enough to meet their subsistence needs and pay their masters but to finance leisure activities.

The range of services performed by slaves on the self-hire system in the Bahamas, like the range of crops produced by slaves on their provision grounds throughout the region, was extensive; from skilled artisans and domestics to unskilled laborers. As Governor Smyth remarked in 1832, "it has long been a custom in this Colony to permit the more intelligent of the Slaves, & more particularly Artificers, to find employment for themselves & to pay to their owners either the whole or such a proportion of what they may gain as may be agreed upon between the Parties" (ibid., 39). Indeed, "at Nassau almost all the mechanics, & even the seafaring people are slaves, who pay a fixed sum to their owners, & make what they can by their labour" (ibid., 37).[17] It can not be stressed enough that the self-hire system was voluntary; slaves not wanting to operate under it could still make claims on their owners for rations. Even so, many Bahamian slaves eagerly exploited this practice to their advantage.

Johnson (1996) argues that their experiences with self-hire eased the transition of blacks in the Bahamas from slavery to freedom. Indeed, after slavery many West Indians remained on the plantation or became "free" peasants. Rather than slaves they became tenants; the rhythms of life only barely changing. In Trinidad and Barbados, for instance, plantations remained the principle unit of economic organization. And, in Jamaica, freedmen "repudiating [their] previous status as an estate laborer" became peasants growing enough for subsistence and marketing whatever surplus resulted from their efforts (Mintz and Hall 1970, 23). Most Caribbean economies, therefore, have remained principally plantation economies (Levitt and Best 1975). In the Bahamas, however, little or no attempt was made by plantation owners after emancipation to eke out a living on their farms by hiring their former slaves as paid laborers. As Albury (1975, 116) suggests, "the sheer difficulty of making ends meet was too much for the planters. One by one, they quitted their land and quitted the Bahamas. By the early 1830s most of them were gone." Additionally, Bahamian slaves on self-hire were unfamiliar with both the subsistence of peasant life and the vagaries of plantation labor.

Although I agree with Johnson's assessment, I conjecture that the uniqueness of the Bahamian variant should not only be credited with easing the transition out of slavery but with laying the foundation for an economic system altogether different than the plantation economies found throughout the West Indies. The self-hire system fundamentally altered the trajectory of the Bahamian economy. Because of the uniqueness of the self-hire system, slavery in the Bahamas got dismantled in an entirely different way and at an entirely different speed than it did in other Caribbean colonies. The uniqueness of the Bahamas' system of slavery should also be credited with cementing the belief that *enterprise could lead to economic success* into the Bahamian consciousness. And, with creating a festival (the semi-annual Junkanoo celebrations) and culture (the Junkanoo ethos) where hard work and creativity are celebrated.

Rushin' as Entrepreneurship

Junkanoo is a carnival like festival that takes place in the early morning hours of Boxing Day (the day after Christmas) and New Year's Day. Groups of revelers *rush* down Bay Street, historically the main commercial strip in Nassau, adorned in colorful costumes made of crepe paper and cardboard, beating goat skin drums (called Goombay drums) or shaking cowbells, and blowing whistles, conch shells, bugles or (more recently) playing brass instruments like the trumpet or the trombone.[18] The constant droning of the Goombay drums change the rhythm of your heart and foreigners and Bahamians alike find it impossible to stand still while the parade is passing by.

The African origins of Junkanoo are without question. Wood (1995, 3), for instance, has remarked that "one of the most vibrant examples of Bahamian culture with African roots is Junkanoo." Although the timing of the festival and perhaps the style of costumes and possibly some of the practices are due to the vagaries of life in the Bahamas (as a British colony), at its core and from the beginning Junkanoo was an African rooted celebration. As Craton and Saunders (1998, 488) contend, "from . . . African roots came the goombay drums and rhythm, masks, horns, staves, and stilts, and the central figure of Pitchy-Patchy, alias John Canoe; from England . . . the mumming tradition of . . . caroling for handouts . . .; and from the slave plantation culture, the seasonal largesse, permitted license, and satiric role reversals of the turn-of-the-year holiday." Bahamian Junkanoo, as Wood (1995, 3) reports, "grew out the celebrations of enslaved people in the eighteenth and nineteenth centuries, when they had three days off at Christmas, and were relatively free during that period to pursue their own entertainment." Not surprisingly then, several links can be drawn between "the early character" of Bahamian Junkanoo and "similar festivals throughout the former British slave colonies acquired before 1763, that is, those that were not formerly French or Spanish (whose official religion was Roman Catholic) and therefore developed the very distinct alternative tradition of

Carnival" (ibid.). Junkanoo in the Bahamas, as such, thus shares a common heritage (and has much in common) with Jamaican Jonkonnu, Belizean John Canoe, the now defunct North Carolina John Kuner celebrations and the Gombeys of Bermuda.

But, just as slavery in the Bahamas (as we have seen) was quite distinct from slavery elsewhere in the Caribbean, the disparate social and economic history of the Bahamas caused Junkanoo to evolve in a way quite distinct from its cousins throughout the region. As Craton and Saunders (1998, 488) argue,

> The most important of these formative features were five in number: [1] the absence of a prolonged and intensive plantation economy and the consequent opportunities for the black majority to sustain and develop their own traditions; [2] the increasing concentration of the population on the metropolitan island of New Providence, which alone had the resources to develop a full-fledged festival; [3] the spatial separation of commercial, bourgeois, white elite, and brown middle-class downtown Nassau (where Junkanoo was performed) from the predominantly poor and black Over the Hill suburbs (where Junkanoo was prepared and rehearsed); [4] the early formalization of the parades as a legitimized, if tightly controlled, spectacle-confrontation; [5] and, finally, the revivifying influence of the intermittent immigration from 1811 to 1860 . . . of thousands of liberated Africans, the last of whom did not die until well into the twentieth century.

Junkanoo is perhaps the purest transmission/representation of the culture that blacks in the Bahamas developed during slavery. Much of what was created (and retained from Africa) in the space that slaves were able to carve out because of their access to provision plots and free time, is embedded in this annual ritual and transmitted by the practices and attitudes that surround this celebration. Junkanoo is more than just a festival that signals the beginning and end of the Bahamian year.

Junkanoo, or rather the spirit of Junkanoo, exists as the core of what it means to be Bahamian. Craton and Saunders (1998, 488), for instance, has called Junkanoo "the essential expression of Bahamian identity" and, as one Junkanooer remarked, "a Bahamian has Junkanoo in him" (Wood 1995, 19). Indeed, Junkanoo is the quintessential Bahamian cultural experience and, as such, understanding Junkanoo, not only, that is, what it means to be on Bay Street New Year's morning but, also, what it means to hear/feel the rhythm of Junkanoo even in May or June and the lessons learnt during the almost year long preparation for each Junkanoo parade, is, therefore, critical to understanding Bahamian culture and what it means to be a Bahamian. As Ferguson (2000, 2) suggests, "To Bahamians, it is a most natural part of life, as vital, energizing, and soul quenching as water."

Arlene Nash Ferguson's colorful description of the excitement in the various Junkanoo *shacks* (where the costumes are created) in the days leading up a Junkanoo parade is quite revealing and speaks to the central place that Junkanoo holds in the hearts of Bahamians. As Ferguson (2000, 30) reports,

> It was like coming home again after a long absence. And everyone coming through the door said the same thing: 'I come to get me!' They meant that they had come to get their costumes.
>
> 'I come to get me.' I felt a tinge stir in my chest. With those words, the door to our heritage had slowly opened again, and our forefathers were reaching out across the centuries, bequeathing a proud and indomitable heritage through the power of Junkanoo. There was in those of us called to carry on the tradition, the subconscious realization that Junkanoo was the place to keep our souls. The real 'me' would emerge in our costumes, the colours of our character, the design of our personalities, the pattern of our tastes, our pride, and our signature. On Bay, in our costumes, we would feel complete.
>
> Within this crude, unfinished building [the Junkanoo shack] was the bridge to the past, confirmation of the proud story heard at my grandparents' knees. This ancient ritual that we had begun again was a gift from our ancestors, an annual renewal of self. In going to Bay each year, we would now reverse the trend of History and joyously proclaim the triumph of the Bahamian spirit: parade it in the intricate steps of the dance, thunder it from the pounding of our drums, shout it in the sound of our cowbells.

So, what are some of the beliefs embedded in that ritual and which habits are developed during the preparation for the semi-annual celebrations? Indeed, who is that 'me' that Ferguson and the other revelers have gone to get in preparation for the festival?

As hinted at before, Junkanoo, like the B' Bouki and B' Rabbi folk tales, colors the way Bahamians view entrepreneurship and affects the way they do business. Perhaps the most important lesson that Junkanoo teaches is that success is possible through effort; the work ethic that attends Junkanoo resembles the Protestant work ethic that has contributed to the economic success of much of the Western hemisphere. Preparation begins for the two turn-of-the-year parades just a few days after New Year's Day. By mid-January the leaders of the various Junkanoo groups are getting together regularly to discuss themes for the upcoming parades, by March designs for the various costumes are being vetted and by September the Junkanooers are in the *shacks* building costumes and in the parks practicing their music and dance routines. As Wood (1995, 19) reports, "each year from June to the close of the New Year's Day parade Junkanooers direct their energies fully toward the production of costumes and music for the parade." Each parade is a fierce competition between the handful of organized groups, and each Junkanooer knows that success in December is directly related to preparation in June. This culture, I contend, can not help but affect entrepreneurship given the centrality of the Junkanoo experience to the Bahamian psyche. While Bahamian folklore supports a sort of trickster culture (where hard work is ridiculed and getting something for nothing is celebrated), Junkanoo teaches precisely the opposite lesson.

Junkanoo also reminds Bahamians to trust in their own creativity. To be sure, Junkanoo is not entirely homegrown. From the very beginning, Junkanoo was shaped by the Bahamas' contact with British culture and, increasingly, Junkanoo costumes and music are being influenced by Trinidadian and Brazilian carnival. But, Junkanoo is still for the most part a Bahamian operation. The leaders, designers, dancers, costume builders and musicians are all Bahamians. As I have argued elsewhere, creativity is indispensable to entrepreneurship. If Bahamians were to doubt in their creative potential then domestic sources of entrepreneurship are likely to be impeded and/or impaired (Storr 2002). That Bahamian creativity is celebrated in this critical sphere of Bahamian culture is, therefore, likely to have an important affect on entrepreneurship.

Additionally, Junkanoo recasts the relationship that Bahamians have with the fruits of their labor. Marx has complained (convincingly to some) that under capitalism, laborers are alienated from the fruits of their labor, their environment, themselves and each other. And, as Sowell (1985, 34) suggests, "Alienation, in Marx's sense, is not simply a general malaise but more specifically a misconception of reality growing out of thwarted development." Junkanoo, however, turns that notion (that capitalism necessarily leads to alienation) on its head. Although a great deal of money exchanges hands during the year long preparation for the parades,[19] Junkanoo brings Bahamians closer to themselves, their labor and each other. Although it is perhaps possible to argue that this is an example of extreme alienation, for anybody familiar with African and Bahamian cultures it is obvious that this read of what is occurring would be quite mistaken. The Junkanoo costume is not elevated to the status of a god, nor is "human reality and human needs" made "subservient to artificially created things" during the preparation for and celebration of each Junkanoo. Instead, the Junkanoo costume is a symbolic expression of Bahamianess and the Junkanoo experience the quintessential Bahamian experience. Remember that when people come to pick up their costumes (that they have, by the way, paid hundred of dollars to have made), they remark that they have "come to get me." Rather than being alienating then, Junkanoo is instead integrating and, as such, teaches Bahamians that economic relationships (in general) need not be alienating.

So while getting something for nothing and a celebration of cunning over hard work are both symptoms of the trickster culture that most certainly exists in the Bahamas, Junkanoo culture, if you will, celebrates creativity, achievement through hard work and the notion that work need not be alienating but can instead be a pure expression of self. As such, it has had a similarly profound effect on the mode and pattern of entrepreneurship that exists in the Bahamas. The trickster ethos, as we have seen, gave rise to the *master pirate* that has taken up (seemingly) permanent residence in Bahamian waters. The spirit of Junkanoo lives in the *enterprising slave* (the other major character in the Bahamas' economic narrative).[20]

The Enterprising Slave

> Contemporary travellers who were qualified to make comparisons were in general agreement that slaves were treated far better in the Bahamas than elsewhere in the West Indies. But it is a difficult matter to deal with because, however they were treated, they were still slaves.
>
> This was the crux of the matter. Good treatment of slaves was commendable but insignificant compared to the immense evil of the system itself.
>
> Albury (1975, 126)

The Akan symbol, *Sankofa,* teaches us to look at the past in order to understand the present and to construct the future. For a people descended from Akan peoples, looking back is, therefore, a desirable if not instinctive process. Although Thompson (1997) has called their past "haunting," traveling through Caribbean history need not be a perilous journey. We might, for instance, learn a great deal about Bahamians and, indeed, all Caribbean peoples by examining their pasts; even this ugly epoch.

Although slavery was an unmitigated attack on the West Indian of African descent, it failed to defeat him. In spite of an all out effort to make him docile, he remained spirited and vibrant. Amazingly, Caribbean slaves metamorphosed into a proto-peasantry in spite of their chattel status and, even while they were slaves, grew their own provisions and marketed surplus produce and dry goods. Turning the myth that slaves were lazy and shiftless on its head, Caribbean slaves needed neither the eye of the overseer nor the chiding of the whip to be industrious. As one observer remarked, the "African it seems is a most industrious character as will appear from the quantity of provisions he sells" (quoted in Johnson 2000).

Higglerism in the Bahamas, however, has a peculiar tinge to it. While the Bahamas' experience with piracy gave rise to the *master pirate,* the peculiarity of Bahamian slavery and the presence of a large population of free and materially well-to-do blacks in the Bahamas gave birth to the *enterprising slave* (an equally prominent figure in the economic story of the Bahamas). Tales of blacks attaining success through their labor are not unfamiliar tales in the Bahamas. Unlike the *master pirate*, the *enterprising slave* succeeds not through her wiles but through her work. She is not a trickster, but a laborer. Her chief characteristic is, thus, her belief that success through hard work is possible even in the face of extreme obstacles. In this, she is not at all like her chief rival (who eschews ordinary returns and prefers something for nothing). The next chapter tries to contend with the presence of these seemingly incompatible characters and irreconcilable types of entrepreneurs in Bahamian markets.

Notes

[1] GDP per capita (constant 1995 US dollars) in 2000 was $13, 928 in the Bahamas, $8, 876 in Antigua, $8, 282 in Barbados, $2, 115 in Jamaica and $ 934 in Guyana (World Bank, 2002 World Development Indicators).

[2] The *Code noir* (the Royal Edict of 1685 which governed slavery in the French colonies), for instance, insisted that masters be "totally responsible for the maintenance of [their] slaves" (Tomich ([1990] 1991, 306). In contrast, the laws in Jamaica mandated that slaves only be given alternate Saturdays to tend to their provision plots. Slavery as practiced in the region did not conform to either law.

[3] The 1661 *Barbadian Slave Act*, which was eventually exported to the rest of the British Caribbean, was more often "honored in the breach" than in the observance. As Mintz (1993, 96) remarks, "we may be sure of a number of general characteristics of Caribbean slave systems: the formal slave codes never represented, other than very superficially, the actual character of life in each society; each island society differed in certain important ways from every other, with regard to its treatment of the slave population; and in each and every system, the slaves were able to work out certain creative adaptations, in spite of the profoundly repressive conditions under which they were forced to live."

[4] As Beckles (1990, 34) explains, "this meant that slaves were legally tied to plantations, and could not easily be alienated from them in probate settlements."

[5] As Johnson (2000, 46) explains, "slaves created a society over time that clearly bore the stamp of Africa, although the society was not purely African."

[6] This is true even though slaves in the British West Indies were not formally given the right to market their wares until 1735. The 1735 law permitted slaves to "carry about, and sell, all manner of provisions, fruits, fresh fish, milk poultry, and other

small stock of all kinds, having a ticket from their owner or employer" (Long 1774 cited in Mintz and Hall 1970, 15).

[7] Interestingly, on market day many of the restrictions which governed the movements of slaves between plantations and back and forth to the town were relaxed. And, reports of slaves traveling great distances to attend this or that market are quite common.

[8] Some controversy exists about the role *slaves* played in these weekend markets. Knight (1990, 119), for instance, makes the claim that "the internal marketing system was dominated by free persons of color. Slaves participated too, but during the eighteenth century, a series of laws gradually proscribed their economic activities." That *de jure* restrictions on the market activities of slaves existed, however, says little about the enforcement or the success of those prohibitions. As we know from the record, much of the practices that I discussed in this study existed in opposition to the laws that were on the books. Also, that these laws to "proscribe" the market activities of slaves were desired in the first place, suggests that the practices they hoped to curtail were in fact taking place.

[9] As Wylly reported to the 1815 *House of Assembly Enquiry into the Condition of Slaves and Free Blacks,* "besides the stated allowance of grain, to which our plantation Negroes are by law entitled, they are allowed as much ground as they choose to cultivate, and are universally permitted to raise hogs and poultry . . . They sell them all" (Cash, et al,1991, 205).

[10] Like their cousins in Jamaica, Barbados and Trinidad, planters in the Bahamas also felt threatened by the market activities of Bahamian slaves and tried to curtail them. The 1767 *Act for the Governing of Negroes, Mulattoes and Indians,* for instance, stated that "no person or persons shall presume to trade with any Negro or other slave either in buying, selling or bartering without the leave or consent of the owner of such Negro . . . which consent shall be in writing . . . specifying the quantity or quality of the articles he or she is allowed to sell" (Cash, et al, 1991, 186).

[11] Also, see Craton and Saunders (1992, 319).

[12] Consider, for instance, slave life on Lord Rolle's Exuma estate in the 1790s. As Craton and Saunders (1992, 314) report, "though turned out to the fields each day at 6:30 A.M, nearly all slaves had finished their tasks and were back in their huts by 1 P.M., ready to work their own grounds, to look after their stock, go fishing, or simply relax."

[13] As McKinnen (cited in Cash, et al, 1991, 192) explains, "The *tasks* are one fourth of an acre in extent; they are usually marked out by permanent stations in every field, and two, three, sometimes four slaves (but in general more than one) are put into each task."

[14] Consider, for instance, the way Bahamian slaves were treated on fishing expeditions. Reportedly, Bahamian slaves who served on fishing vessels earned the

same shares as their white shipmates. Slaves elsewhere could not imagine being employed on equal terms as white laborers.

[15] Indeed, in the late 18th and early 19th centuries, the Bahamas (particularly New Providence) had a large population of free blacks; some had been manumitted but many had never been slaves. In 1807, the British government decided to garrison the Bahamas with regiments of black soldiers. And, in the aftermath of the abolition of the slave trade, hundreds of Africans who were freed from illegal slave ships were settled in the Bahamas. As Johnson (2000, 112) describes, "between 1811 and 1828, approximately 1,102 liberated Africans were brought to the Bahamas."

[16] The support that Johnson (1996) offers for this assertion is quite compelling. As such Craton ([1962] 1986, 185) is simply mistaken when he asserts that it was not until 1826 that slaves "could be given permission to open up trade in dry goods" and that it was then that "slaves began to use money for the first time."

[17] Governor Smyth's openness is quite dissimilar from the efforts (admittedly often frustrated) in Barbados to prevent slaves from becoming skilled laborers. As Dunn (1972, 242) reports, "In 1676 Barbados Negroes were prohibited from entering such skilled crafts as cooper, smith, carpenter, tailor, or boatman, so as to reserve these occupations for Christian artisans."

[18] *Rushin'* is the colloquialism for participating in a Junkanoo parade.

[19] Groups can spends upwards to $150, 000 per parade on supplies and labor (costume builders).

[20] By maintaining that Bahamian entrepreneurs are in many respects like *enterprising slaves,* I am not intending to be offensive; I am aware that the term slave has always and continues to have severe negative connotations. I use it here, however, because it (a) reminds us how and when this ideal type emerged and (b) it also suggests that the *enterprising spirit* that fills Bahamians is still proscribed in many ways (a number of constraints still make it difficult for individual Bahamian entrepreneurs to translate their efforts into any real economic success). See Butkevich and Storr (2001) and Storr (2002) for a discussion of some of these constraints.

Chapter Five

Competing Metaphors: Explaining Enterprise in the Bahamas

Introduction

Bahamians (particularly entrepreneurs) suffer from something akin to what Lamming has called a *fractured consciousness*. Describing the deleterious effects that colonialism and slavery have had on the West Indian psyche, Lamming (1983, xxxvii) has argued that the result was, "a deep split in [the West Indian's] sensibility which ... raised difficult problems of language and values; the whole issue of cultural allegiance between the imposed norms of White Power, represented by a small numerical minority, and the fragmented memory of the African masses: between White instruction and Black imagination." Colonialism and slavery, you should remember, were amongst other things psychological conquest.[1] Blacks were brutalized (under both systems) and taught horrible lessons regarding their supposed inferiority and inadequacies.

The legacy of colonialism, thus, forces West Indian blacks to cope with two distinct and often contradictory world views (one of African inferiority presented against a pre-existing backdrop an innate African self-esteem). And so, forces them and subsequently their descendants to come to terms with "the totalitarian demands of White supremacy, in a British colony, the psychological injury inflicted by the sacred rule that all forms of social status would be determined by the degrees of skin complexion; the ambiguities among Blacks themselves about the credibility of their own spiritual history" (ibid.).[2] Du Bois ([1903] 1969) has made a similar argument concerning the impact that slavery and Jim Crowism has had on the consciousness of American blacks. As Du Bois ([1903] 1969, 45) suggests,

> The Negro [the Afro-American] is a sort of seventh son, born with a veil, and gifted with second-sight in this American world, – a world which yields him no true self-consciousness, but only lets him see himself through the revelation of the other world. It is a peculiar sensation, this double-consciousness, this sense of always looking at one's self through the eyes of others, of measuring one's soul by the tape of a world that looks on in amused contempt and pity. One ever feels his twoness, – an American, a Negro; two souls, two thoughts, two unreconciled strivings; two warring ideals in one dark body, whose dogged strength alone keeps it from being torn asunder.

Although the twoness, the two souls, the double-consciousness that, I contend, plagues Bahamian entrepreneurs is somewhat different than the competing consciousnesses that typically plague Africans in the U.S. and the Americas, a definite link should be drawn between the arguments concerning the two orientations to entrepreneurship that color Bahamian business practices (presented here) and Du Bois' and Lamming's well established and accepted articulations of "schizophrenia" in the Diaspora.[3]

The Bahamas' socio-economic history and its unique cultural milieu have given Bahamian entrepreneurs two dissimilar (and often opposing) metaphors for doing business and have resulted in the evolution of two distinct ideal types of the Bahamian entrepreneur. As Craton and Saunders (1992, 104) suggests,

> Piracy stands for the opposite pole in the Bahamian lifestyle and character from that implanted by farming, fishing, and other respectable pursuits. But there has rarely been a clearcut or permanent division, even at the individual level within a single lifetime. Rather, there has always been an almost schizophrenic tendency to crossover, particularly when there has

> been a recurrence of the conditions of extreme poverty, lack of profitable alternatives, and the absence of strong forces of law and order found during the classic era of Bahamian piracy.

Both the *master pirate* (that evolved because of the Bahamas' pirate past) and the *enterprising slave* (which burgeoned even under slavery) are alive and well in the Bahamas. While getting something for nothing and a celebration of cunning over hard work are characteristics of the *master pirate,* you might recall, the *enterprising slave,* on the other hand, relies on his own creativity and believes that achievement (even extraordinary achievement) through hard work is possible. What, then, are some of the business practices that flow from the presence of these two competing figures? How have they influenced business life in the Bahamas?

Understanding Bahamian Business Practices

> In this country, you are not considered upwardly mobile unless you are demonstrably, visibly and even vulgarly so.
>
> The short route to upward mobility in The Bahamas is to take up an occupation that allows you to overcharge or bilk your clients without the fear of the law common criminals are forced to have.
>
> Glinton-Meicholas (1998, 40)
>
> Bahamians have an extraordinary yen and flair for entrepreneurship and all the necessary optimism. Our people will open little shops or roadside stalls with little more than a hope, a prayer and a price list.
>
> Glinton-Meicholas (1994, 65)

Patricia Glinton-Meicholas often writes truths that Bahamians wished went unuttered. In her poignant series *How to Be a True-True Bahamian,* for instance, Glinton-Meicholas informs that Bahamians have an "egocentric" world view "shaped by island geography ... many of us see the planet Earth as the centre of all creation, The Bahamas as the centre of Earth, and each Bahamian sees him or herself as the shining light of our country" (Glinton-Meicholas 1998, 5). That Bahamian businessmen often resemble the mobility motivated people she describes above is a similarly uncomfortable confession. Uncomfortable but true. As true as her contention that many Bahamian businessmen tend to be optimistic, enterprising figures. As is clear from a careful read of Glinton-Meicholas' work, neither the *master pirate* nor the *enterprising slave* is a wholly dominant figure in the Bahamas. Like a child, which often looks (at least a little bit) like each of her parents, Bahamian businessmen often exhibit traits that are attributable to each of these guiding figures. Indeed, Bahamian businessmen are seldom wholly *piratical* or purely *enterprising*. Even so, I believe that it is fair to align particular practices with one way of viewing business rather than the other; to say, for instance, that one set of practices are more closely associated with the *master pirate* than the *enterprising slave* and vice versa.

Remember, for instance, that I have described the *master pirate* as necessarily having a narrow radius of trust. As I noted, pirates and smugglers who were too trusting in their business dealings risked not only their livelihood but their lives. Consistent with their pirate past, Bahamians tend to be low-trust when it comes to their business dealings even though they exhibit high levels of trust elsewhere.[4] Consider, for example, Glinton-Meicholas' (1998) description of how Bahamians learn and inform others of job vacancies. As she (ibid., 112) suggests,

> When Bahamians . . . learn of or have the power to make the selection for a job vacancy, they immediately begin to canvas their memories for connections who may be looking for work. As always they begin with the inner core of all that is important – themselves. If it is not a position which could provide promotion for them, they will pass news of the opportunity on to their nearest and dearest, and move outward. They will jealously guard the information, do all they can to win favour for any applications relatives or friends have submitted, until all kith and kin have refused. Only then will knowledge of the job become public.

As a consequence (and a possible cause) of the nepotism Glinton-Meicholas describes above, Bahamian workers not related to their employers often feel only minimally attached and loyal to them.[5]

In addition, as is common in countries where businessmen exhibit a narrow radius of trust, private firms in the Bahamas tend to be small while most of the larger operations in the country are foreign or state owned.[6] In the Bahamas, for instance, the state owns the only telephone company, the only local television station, one of the two existing power companies, three of the four existing hospitals, one of the few airline companies that services the less popular islands in the country and has often been a big investor in hotels and agriculture. That Bahamian *pirate* entrepreneurs have narrow radiuses of trust even though the Bahamas can not be reasonably classified as a low-trust society and the resultant nepotism and predominance of small, hierarchically organized, family firms that attends Bahamian businesses, are not, however, the only consequences of the Bahamas' pirate past.

Recall, I have argued that our ever-present *master pirate* can also be accused of being impatient, that is, of having a high time preference. Savings rates tend to be lower in the Bahamas than they are in other West Indian contexts. Bahamians, for instance, save only 11% of their annual gross domestic product (on average over the last four years for which we have data (1989-1992); Inter-American Development Bank: Statistics and Quantitative Analysis Unit). Compare this to 16.83% in Barbados, 24.65% in Jamaica and 25.5 % in Trinidad (for the same period; ibid.). This is true even though many of the traditional explanations of low (and relatively low) savings rates are not, however, applicable: the Bahamas has always had a stable democratic government, central bank interference into the banking sector is minimal, the government levels no taxes on interest income and the Bahamas has had relatively low levels of inflation (inflation in the Bahamas was on par with U.S. inflation in each of the last ten years; The Central Bank of the Bahamas: Quarterly Statistical Digest February 2000).

I contend that this high time preference, this high preference for current over future consumption that I have associated with the *master pirate,* explains why (a) poor customer service, (b) a predominance of low-capital intensive industries and (c) politicized business relationships are common features of business life in the Bahamas. Customer service in the Bahamas is indeed poor. As Glinton-Meicholas (1998, 117) contends,

> At a certain level of the workforce, the customer becomes the enemy, whom you will refer to as 'these people'. These people will keep you in a constant state of annoyance, because their demands for service will force you to work. To pay them back for troubling your life, you will do all in your power to frustrate their plans.
>
> When [Bahamian workers] are finally forced to begin receiving customers, [they] will make sure that neither by word or deed [they] allow anybody to think that [that they] are glad to be of service. [They] will not return greetings, nor look any customer in the eye. When [they] do, it will be to give that person the slow, sideways shutting of the eyes which Bahamians . . . [use] to show contempt or general ill will.[7]

Arguably, employers only allow employees to "get away" with this sort of behavior because establishing goodwill requires an investment (training, wage incentives, etc.) that they are often unwilling to make.[8]

The high discount rate (the consequence of a short-term time horizon) often held by Bahamian entrepreneurs also discourages investment in businesses that will only become profitable well into the future.[9] This is because the higher the discount rate, the lower the present value of all dollars that will be earned in the future. And, the lower the present value of expected profits from an enterprise, the less likely it is that individuals will invest in it. As such, capital intensive industries are seldom launched (particularly by Bahamians) in the Bahamas.[10] Remember, the *master pirate* is on the look out for the quickest route to prosperity (his is a desire to profiteer not profit) and that "the short route to upward mobility in The Bahamas is to take up an occupation that allows you to overcharge or bilk your clients without the fear of the law common criminals are forced to have" (Glinton-Meicholas 1998, 40). Bahamians, thus, tend to invest in restaurants, salons, clothing stores and other retail or service oriented companies and not in large-scale manufacturing or commercial agriculture.[11]

The politicization of the economy is, arguably, also a consequence of the high-time preference of the *master pirate*. Profiteering is not only about earning profits quickly but about earning extra-ordinary profits, as well. Rent seeking, in virtually every context, tends to yield abnormally high returns in relatively short periods of time. This is particularly true in the Bahamas where, "the surest way to prominence and wealth . . . is through active participation in politics" (Glinton-Meicholas 1998, 69). Indeed, under the Pindling administrations of the 1970s and 1980s, it was not uncommon for Members of Parliament to own companies that did business either exclusively or primarily with the government. Reports of government corruption (even at the Cabinet level) were also quite common during the 25 years that Pindling was Premier[12] and in 1990 the Bahamas was listed as one of the six most corrupt countries in the world (Easterly 2001, 245).[13]

While the *master pirate* can be "accused" of encouraging the narrow radius of trust and high time preference that plagues business dealings in the Bahamas, the *enterprising slave,* as suggested earlier, can be credited with encouraging the *spirit of enterprise* that is also a common trait of Bahamian entrepreneurs. As Glinton-Meicholas (1994, 64) reports, "Bahamians have an extraordinary yen and flair for entrepreneurship and all of the necessary optimism." Although Rabbyism (the "something for nothing" ethos) is prevalent in the Bahamas, many Bahamians have a strong work ethic. And, although many of the successful industries in the Bahamas have been piratical in nature, Bahamians have not shied away from industries that require hard labor. Over the years, for example, Bahamians have labored as field hands, spongers, sisal farmers and today many still eke out a living as subsistence farmers.

Remember, "work ethics" come from a variety of sources; Protestantism in the West, a sense of obligation in Japan, Junkanoo and the peculiar experience of slavery in the Bahamas. Similarly, "work ethics" also come in a variety of different flavors. Not surprisingly then, the animating spirit behind Bahamian businesses is quite distinct from the enterprising spirits found elsewhere. The asceticism consistent with the Protestant ethic, for instance, is not present in the Bahamas. As Glinton-Meicholas (1998, 40) suggests, "in this country, you are not considered upwardly mobile unless you are demonstrably, visibly and even vulgarly so."

Bahamian entrepreneurship is also buttressed by a number of institutions that are African in origin and so closely aligned with the *enterprising slaves* that dominate economic life in the Bahamas. One such institution is *asue*. As Glinton-Meicholas (1995, 16) describes,

> The asue is a collective savings or loan plan by which Bahamians accumulate large sums to make special purchases or payments. No banks are involved, and participants make a specified contribution for a specified period to a pool kept by the 'asue-keeper'. Each person is assigned a 'draw', or a time in which he or she collects the total pool. When you hear people say 'I get my asue draw', they mean that they have collected.

Called *susu* or *esusu* in Ghana and other African and Caribbean contexts, these rotating credit relationships encourage savings and are a valuable financial resource; particularly, for small scale entrepreneurs.[14]

Also, it is as true today as it was during those Sunday markets that were common in the 18th and 19th centuries, that "a permanent location" is not a requirement for becoming a successful haggler in the Bahamas. As Glinton-Meicholas (1994, 67) describes,

> The award winner in this category? The Bahamian vendors who sell lunches from the trunk or boot of their cars. The marvel is that, from this small space, they can serve up a variety of entrees, soups, salads, desserts and beverages. These mobile restaurateurs can take their operations to the customer. They can be found stationed wherever large numbers of hungry people gather: on the docks near fish and fruit sellers, in the carparks of large office buildings and especially at construction sites.

The ingenuity and color, the hustle and resourcefulness, the *succeed-despite-obstacles* ethos that makes Junkanoo "an event to remember" also affects (or perhaps I should say infects) business life in the Bahamas. The *enterprising slave*, whether he is a "peanut boy" or a straw vendor or a shopkeeper or a restaurateur, is a capable, creative creature.

As I suggested earlier, however, neither figure, neither the *enterprising slave* nor the *master pirate* exists wholly independent of the other. Characteristics associated with the *master pirates* and traits more closely aligned with the *enterprising slaves* are often found (indeed are necessarily found albeit to different degrees) in every Bahamian entrepreneur. Perhaps the clearest example of the interplay of these two (sometimes) "warring" characters can be seen in the emergence and development of the 99¢ breakfast industry in the middle to the late 1990s. As Glinton-Meicholas (1998, 102-103) describes in detail,

> In about 1996 or 1997, an enterprising Bahamian went one better in the usual mobile Bahamian restaurant theme. He or she had a miniscule clapboard cottage built on wheeled base. Transporting this structure daily to a vacant lot near a busy intersection, the owner opened shop advertising a 99¢ breakfast to instant success.
>
> Before you could say 'Kukamakai!' wave a magic wand or twinkle an eye, the 99¢ venture was imitated all over town . . .
>
> Now here is a mystery. How does a cheap breakfast and widespread imitation fit into the picture . . . of the Lexus, Rolex-loving and egotistical Bahamian? Very well.
>
> The answer to the 99¢ meal is that [it] smacks of getting something over a fellow Bahamian. The imitation? Why its not imitation at all. I can take the same business idea, wear the same clothing and speak the same clichés and do it all better than anyone has ever done it before.
>
> Don't think that creativity is infrequent among Bahamians. The truth is that we prefer to practice mental and muscular economy. Let someone else do the taxing groundwork and we will stand ready to dash into the magnesium flash of success at the end.

Evident in this account is both the ingenuity and hard work that attends the Bahamas' Junkanoo culture as well as the cunning (the "something for nothing" ethos) that is often times celebrated in Bahamian folklore.

The *master pirate* and the *enterprising slave* have not only thrived in the Bahamas but the Bahamas has thrived as a result of their efforts. The Bahamas is the richest country in the West Indies. In the Bahamas, GDP per capita (in constant 1995 US$) was just under $14,000 in 2000. Compare that to the figures for Antigua ($8,876), the next richest, as well as, Barbados ($8,282), Trinidad ($5,324) and Jamaica ($2,115) (World Bank, 2002 World Development Indicators). Similarly, unemployment in the Bahamas was only 8% (of the total work force) in 1999 compared to 10% in Barbados, 13% in Trinidad and 16% in Jamaica (ibid.). Much of the Bahamas' recent economic success has been on the strength of two of the Bahamas' leading industries: Tourism and Off-Shore Banking. How have the *master pirate* and the *enterprising slave* fared in these particular endeavors? How have these industries affected and been affected by the two primary metaphors for doing business in the Bahamas?

Selling Paradise and Burying Treasure

Tourism and Offshore Banking are vastly important industries in the Bahamas. Indeed, the size and scope of these two industries, thus, makes them impossible to ignore when considering economic life in the Bahamas. Drawn to beautiful beaches with crystal clear water that crawls up (never crashes against) the pearl colored sand so common in the Bahamas, some four million tourists pass through Bahamian waters annually. Although over 60% of these tourists visit the Bahamas as a part of a cruise and so stay in the Bahamas for only a short time (often under a day), about one and half million (c 35%) of them are so-called "stop-over" visitors. Not surprisingly then, tourism is a billion dollar industry in the Bahamas (in 2000, for instance, tourists spent 1.8 billion US$). While it's the beauty of the Bahamas' natural environment that attracts Americans and Europeans to Bahamian hotels, it's the beauty of its regulatory environment that has attracted their capital to Bahamian banks.

The Bahamian government through the use of capital and exchange controls has created an "offshore space" that is "insulated and isolated from the domestic sector and [as a consequence] allowed to operate in an almost free environment" (Virgill 2001, 17). Attracted to this paradise where there are no taxes on income and where, until recently, there was only a modicum of regulation, about 300 billion dollars in foreign held assets found their way into Bahamian off-shore banks in 2001. The Offshore sector employs about one thousand Bahamians and contributes over one hundred and fifty million dollars to the domestic product of the Bahamas.

Like all Bahamian economic endeavors, I contend, the look and feel, the structure and success of the Bahamas' tourist and off-shore banking industries has much to do with the two dominant figures in the Bahamian economic narrative.

Evading and Laundering: The Offshore Banking Product

The modern offshore banking system emerged in the 1940s and 50s when "the central banks of the communist block countries determined that their traditional practice of holding their U. S. dollar denominated external reserves on deposit with New York banks, left them open to extreme political and financial risk" (Higgins 1994, 65). As the Cold War heated up, these central banks believed that there was a growing likelihood that their U.S. denominated assets held in American institutions would be seized or frozen by the American government and so they began to deposit their U.S. dollar balances with banks in London or Paris.

The U.S. government gave an additional boost to the Euro-dollar market in the 1960s when, in an attempt to combat its balance of payments difficulties, it imposed a series of regulations affecting the foreign dealings of U.S. firms and citizens (including increased taxes and restrictions on lending to non-Americans). The *Interest Equalization Tax* of 1963, for instance, "made it unattractive for Americans to invest in non-American securities" (Francis 1987, 108). Similarly, *Regulation Q*, imposed by the Federal Reserve Board, "made it unattractive for non-Americans to buy American domestic dollar bonds by limiting the interest rates on these bonds to a level below that of international rates. This made it very difficult for commercial banks to borrow on the American money market" (ibid.). Corporations and banks located within the United States responded by establishing branches or subsidiaries overseas, substantially increasing the Euro-dollar market (ibid.).

Although London has been at the epicenter of this Euro-dollar market from its advent, the Bahamas has been a major player in this sector since the late 1960s. Indeed, offshore banking is now the country's second largest export. As Higgins (1994, 68) suggests,

> The reasons for the success of the Bahamas as an offshore center are many and varied. It was cheaper to operate in the Bahamas than in London and it was geographically closer for United States banks. It had the same English Common Law legal system as both Britain and the United States as well as it shared the same language. The legal system provided for no direct taxation, no exchange controls on non-residents, and bank secrecy provisions for the protection of client confidentiality . . . [and] the Bahamas had a history of relative political and economic stability with a parliamentary democracy and a currency on par with the U. S. dollar.

The offshore banking sector has grown considerably since the first offshore bank was established in the Bahamas in 1936. Indeed, there are now some 379 offshore banks in the Bahamas.[15] As Francis (1987, 108) suggests, "while . . . external factors helped to establish and, indeed, spurred the growth of offshore banking in The Bahamas, it was internal factors that facilitated its development."

The demand for the Bahamian offshore banking product can thus be seen "as a demand for a banking product not subject to investment restrictions, interest rate ceilings or excessive taxes on either depositors' interest income or through required reserves which act as a tax on banks' operations" (Virgill 2001, 20). The U.S. dollar balances that find their way into Bahamian offshore accounts are, for the most part, seeking refuge from the regulations and restrictions (particularly taxes) that are common in other contexts. In many respects, then, offshore banking is just another *piratical* Bahamian industry. Like blockade running and rum smuggling, offshore banking gives non-Bahamians an opportunity to use the Bahamas to skirt foreign laws and so avoid foreign legal prohibitions. At its best, the Bahamas' offshore banking environment gives foreign investors an opportunity to avoid taxes in their home contexts and to bank in a relatively free regulatory environment. At its worst, it gives them an opportunity to launder funds earned through so-called illicit and illegal activities.[16]

The Bahamas was one of the 15 offshore jurisdictions listed in June 2000 as "non-cooperative" with regards to their attempts to combat money laundering by the Financial Action Task Force (an intergovernmental body). It was also one of the 35 offshore centers labeled as a "harmful tax haven" by the Organization for Economic Cooperation and Development (OECD).[17] Although no one really knows how much money is laundered every year, Walker (1999) estimates that about 68 billion dollars of laundered money ends up in the Bahamas every year.[18] As Virgill (2001, 3) suggests, "the term 'offshore banking' usually conjures up thoughts of dubious and illegal banking practices or badly regulated financial systems conducted in unsophisticated Caribbean countries, eager for foreign currencies and revenues and quick to flout international norms and practices." Whether this perception is accurate or not (and there is much to make us believe that it is inaccurate), it is incontrovertible that the bankers, lawyers and businessmen associated with this sector are, thus, principally engaged in the business of hiding (legitimate or illicit) profits, of burying treasure.[19]

The *master pirate* is not, however, the only Bahamian figure engaged in this industry; much of the characteristics associated with the *enterprising slave* are also evidenced by employees in this sector. Although many of the offshore banks in the Bahamas are essentially paper entities and many of jobs that are associated with this industry are manned by expatriates, this industry does employ over one thousand of the hardest working, best educated, better paid members of the Bahamas' labor force. Indeed, one of the reasons that the industry thrives in the Bahamas is because Bahamians possess a skill set (particularly in law and accounting) that "meshes" with the needs of the industry (Higgins 1994, 68). Incidentally, salaries in the offshore banking sector are as high as they are in any segment of the economy.

In 2000, the average salary in the industry was over fifty-three thousand U.S. dollars (compare that to an average salary of thirty-nine thousand in the domestic banking sector).

Banking in general and off-shore banking in particular have, thus, been extremely important to the growth and development of the Bahamian economy. Remember, almost a thousand Bahamians are employed in this industry at above average salaries. And, those banks that have a presence in the country spend an additional $100 million a year in the Bahamas on administrative expenses, staff training and capital structures (Central Bank of the Bahamas, Quarterly Economic Review, March 2002). As important as off-shore banking is and has been to the Bahamas, however, tourism is by far the most important Bahamian industry.

Truth and Lies: The Bahamas' Brochure Discourse

As van der Valk (1979, 94) contends, "tourism is the backbone of the economy of the Bahamas." Tourism is such a major force in the Bahamas that (in spite of the successes in banking) this nation of islands is often (correctly) thought of as a one-trick-pony, as a mono-sector economy. For decades now, over one-third of the Bahamas' total labor force has been directly engaged in tourism and, remember, in 1999 tourism was a 1.5 billion dollar industry (total GDP in 1999 was 4.5 billion in current US$). Tourism is also the largest earner of foreign currency (in a country where so much of its consumer goods are imported) and receipts from tourism represent over 70% of total exports. Additionally, tourism accounts for over half of the taxes and customs duties collected in the Bahamas. Tourism so dominates the Bahamian landscape that Bethel (1989, 129) is perhaps right when he suggests that "like the sun, sand and sea, tourism is considered by the average Bahamian to be a part of the natural order of things."

Although tourism has long been a major industry in the Bahamas, the modern tourist industry began in earnest in the 1950s. Prior to that period, van der Valk (1979, 107) explains, "the Bahamas was poor in natural resources which could be used for profitable economic activities." As he (ibid.) suggested,

> Despite the combination of white coral and beaches, the brilliant sea colours, the clear and mild sea water and the pleasant sunshine these natural resources were not a source of economic activity until some years after World War II when the demand for tourist services started to increase and accelerate.

Valk (1979) offers three reasons for the rapid growth of this industry in the 1950s. The first, a change in the nature of tourist travel or rather the makeup of the ideal-typical tourist, affected tourist industries around the globe. The second and third reasons he offered are peculiar to the Bahamian context.

After World War II, as van der Valk (ibid., 94) contends, leisure travel went from being the purview of only the wealthiest Europeans and Americans (who relocated to warmer climates like the Bahamas for the winter) to an activity accessible to middle and lower income families. As the cost of air travel decreased and the size of disposable incomes increased in Europe and America, the number of tourists visiting places like the Bahamas grew dramatically.

The tourist industry in the Bahamas also profited (and continues to benefit) a great deal, however, from the change to communism in Cuba. After the revolution began in the mid-to-late-1950s, American tourists began to avoid Cuba (en mass) and "a considerable number [of these] came to the Bahamas." As Hepple (2000) argued, "the main stimulus to the tourism industry was the imposition of the trade embargo by the United States government on Cuba in 1961 as a result of Castro's overthrow of the Batista government and his subsequent nationalization of American assets in Cuba."[20] The trade embargo made it impossible (or rather extremely difficult) for Americans to vacation in Cuba; the Bahamas (which is both closer to the United States than is Cuba and closer to Cuba than any other Caribbean country) became a principal alternative.

Admittedly, the Cuban revolution was not the only factor that contributed to the dramatic growth of the Bahamian tourist industry during this period. Another reason that the tourist industry in the Bahamas began to grow rapidly in the 1950s and 1960s was a number of actions by the governments of the day to support the industry (or rather to remove barriers preventing the development of the industry). The 1949 *Hotel Encouragement Act,* for instance, which "provides for customs and other tax benefits to investors . . . attracted foreign private capital and resulted in a rapid expansion of the hotel industry" (van der Valk 1979, 108). Similarly, since the establishment of the Tourism Development Board in c1950 and the Ministry of Tourism in 1964, the Bahamas Government has devoted a great deal of resources to marketing the tourist experience in the Bahamas. As a result of these three developments (the change in the profile of the ideal-typical tourist, the communist revolution in Cuba, and the government's decision to actively support the industry), tourism grew rapidly in the 1950s and 1960s. In 1949, for instance, only 32,000 tourists visited the Bahamas (Heggle 2000), by 1970 over one million tourists were visiting the Bahamas annually.

Although it would be easy to explain the growth of tourism in the Bahamas as resulting entirely from the shocks outlined above, it is incontrovertible that this industry would not have thrived in the Bahamas if Bahamians were not poised to exploit the opportunities that resulted from these changes. If tourism is the engine of the Bahamian economy, then Bahamian entrepreneurs and laborers (both *enterprising slaves* and *master pirates*) are the fuel behind the tremendous growth of the Bahamas' tourist industry. Indeed, many of the sectors of the Bahamian economy associated with the tourist industry rely on the creativity, hard work and *spirit of enterprise* that I have associated with the *enterprising slave.*

As I suggested earlier, the Bahamas' unique experience with slavery (particularly with self-hire) gave the Bahamian people an early introduction to many of the skills necessary to man and operate a service economy. Tourism is perhaps the quintessential service industry. As the brochures all suggest, someone is always there to cater to the vacationer's every need. Be they managers, bellhops, maids, bartenders, waitresses, cooks, security guards, musicians, taxi drivers, or hoteliers, the Bahamians associated with the industry are not about the business of manufacturing goods but are instead trying to make hotels seem like palaces and guests feel like princes and princesses. Since arriving in the Bahamas as slaves, generations of Bahamians have (unfortunately) had experience with this type of endeavor.

Not surprisingly, however, the *master pirate* has also been important to the Bahamas' success in this industry. Recall that the Bahamas only became a leading tourist destination when the U.S. government banned travel to Cuba. And, that Bahamian entrepreneurs and foreign entrepreneurs based in the Bahamas were there, just as they were when the U.S. tried to blockade southern ports, or to prohibit the drinking of alcohol, or to tax profits earned by U.S. firms outside the U.S., to offer an alternative. A consistent theme in the Bahamas' economic story is the readiness of Bahamians (and entrepreneurs based in the Bahamas) to take advantage of the opportunities created by the vagaries of U.S. laws.

Another consistent theme in the Bahamian economic story is the willingness of Bahamian entrepreneurs to use cunning and deception to get ahead. In a country so dominated by tourism, virtually everyone is engaged in or rather must engage in what Strachan (1995), following Walcott (1970), has called a "*brochure discourse*." Indeed, if the country is to remain successful, Bahamians must continue to package their homeland as Paradise, a modern-day Eden, and to behave as if they were the keepers of this Eden. According to Strachan (1995, 2),

> This *brochure discourse* offers an interesting version of "Paradise" to the hungry eye and able pocket book of the foreign vacationer: captivating aerial shots of rocks plunging into deep blue-green waters teeming with colourful fish that flourish amongst astounding coral reefs, a white woman, alone, inviting, walking on a white sand beach without footprints, lush green landscapes, smiling black natives chopping open coconuts, ready to serve, ready to please, gesturing with their hands for you to come and join in the fun.

When Bahamians are not busy creating and perpetuating this fiction of the Bahamas as an exotic paradise, they are, as Strachan (ibid, 4) continues,

> Cultivating a colonial past that adds to the visitors' sense of a quaint island atmosphere. They are keeping alive the Royal Police Marching Band, and preserving the plantation Great Houses. They are refurbishing the seventeenth and eighteenth century forts and singing the exploits of long dead pirates. They are giving tours of the old colonial buildings, giving vacationers rides by horse and carriage, and performing the quadrille while dressed in the style worn by slaves more than a century before (straw hats, scarves and all).

But, this "imagined, heavily promoted, and staged Eden" is quite dissimilar from the real, lived experiences of everyday Bahamians. As Strachan (ibid., 2) suggests, "this world has about as much authenticity for the 'native' as a stage prop or movie backdrop." The "smiling black natives" have real lives that are never represented on the television commercials, or in the marketing pamphlets or in the travel guides. That many live circumscribed lives tainted by soaring crime rates, a dangerous (and seemingly uncontainable) drug trade, political corruption (particularly in the 1970s and 1980s) and now a stagnant economy never makes it into the brochures; government and citizenry alike try to keep these truths hidden.

Indeed, keeping paradise (with all the misrepresentation which that entails) has become a national effort. Arguably it's the Bahamas' recurring experiences with piracy, that is, the view that piracy is a model and metaphor for economic success and the existence of the *master pirate* as one of the two major ideal-typical entrepreneurs in the Bahamas, that has enabled Bahamians to succeed (and succeed wildly) at this charade. At the same time, I contend, the pervasiveness of the "brochure discourse" which necessarily attends tourism also promotes *piracy* and the view that business success requires guile. While it is true that those who succeed in the tourist industry are amongst the hardest working Bahamians around (surviving on tips requires that you hustle), the "brochure discourse" that pervades the industry (and indeed the country) also teaches Bahamians that in the end it is B' Rabbi who succeeds.

Notes

[1] As I, along with my colleague Bridget Butkevich in *Cultural Characters* (2001), contended, "Colonialism it should never be forgotten was conquest. Colonialism did not introduce Africans to the importance of private property; it transformed them into chattel. It did not teach an ungodly people to love God; it introduced them to unimaginable evil. It did not educate an ignorant people, except to teach them horrifying lessons about violence, and oppression, and destruction. The yelping of apologists aside, colonialism was not about civilizing the uncivilized nor was it about teaching the lawless about the rule of law. Instead, colonialism was an all-out attack on the civilizations of Africa and Asia and taught the colonized (perhaps too thoroughly) how laws might be used to brutalize and subjugate the guiltless. Simply, no good came of it. The only thing worse than the havoc that colonialism reaped on African societies, was the damage it did to the psyche of Africans."

[2] See Storr (2002) for a discussion of how colonialism and slavery have colored entrepreneurship in the West Indies. As I argue in that piece, "because of their colonial experience, development in the West Indies has been like driving a car with the emergency break engaged: sluggish."

[3] It is not lost on me that at times the *master pirate* seems an entirely imported, super imposed figure. That, although Bahamians were involved in *piratical* industries, piracy, blockade running and rum smuggling were not Bahamian creations but were principally foreign initiated industries simply based in and hosted by the Bahamas. Meanwhile the *spirit of enterprise* that affects the *enterprising slave* seems totally of the homegrown variety. If this impression is correct, then the links to Du Bois and Lamming are perhaps even more solid than I suggested here.

[4] Although Bahamians exhibit a narrow radius of trust in their business dealings, the Bahamas can not reasonably be characterized as a low-trust society. Indeed, churches, lodges and service clubs thrive in the Bahamas. Fukuyama (1995), in *Trust: The Social Virtues and The Creation of Prosperity*, alerts us to the importance of a country's social capital (for him, social capital includes capabilities "that arise from the prevalence of trust in a society" (ibid., 26) and a community's proclivity for spontaneous sociability). Societies that are rich in social capital, Fukuyama contends, prosper. Low-trust societies do not. Contrary to what is implied by Fukuyama's schema, however, it is not possible to offer unambiguous descriptions of culture. Catchalls like high-trust and low-trust are problematic because cultures may encompass competing themes and, rather than being duplicated intact, cultural attitudes like meanings are "reproduced, negotiated and struggled over." It is possible, therefore,

for a society or an individual, for that matter, to be very trusting in one area and not very trusting in another.

[5] That the path to success depends on "who you know" and not necessarily "what you know" is a familiar theme in Bahamian literature and lore. As Glinton-Meicholas (1998, 120) remarks, "The safe path through all the many passages of life is to 'know a guy' (or a woman). If you ever voice a difficulty that you seem unable to solve, the average Bahamian will ask with sorrowful but suspicious concern, 'Don't you know somebody?'"

[6] As Fukuyama (1995, 30) argues, in low-trust societies there are "a large number of relatively small family firms at one end of the scale, a small number of large state-owned enterprises at the other, and relatively little in between."

[7] Indeed, the customer is not always right in the Bahamas. Bahamian workers will simply not allow themselves to be mistreated even a little bit. As Baker (1998, 57) contends, "Most Bahamians do not tolerate even a hint of condescension. Anyone who treats hotel staff like hired help is likely to be told, 'Don't disrespect me. Make me feel like you know me.'"

[8] In recent years, restaurants in the Bahamas have, unfortunately, begun the practice of automatically adding gratuity to the bill. Although this guarantees that waiters and support staff will be compensated for their service, this undoubtedly has a negative impact on the quality of service provided. And, supervisors in the Bahamas, I contend, often seem more concerned with preventing employee theft (thus the frequent Saturday mornings devoted to doing inventories) than to ensuring that customers receive good service.

[9] Recall that the narrow radius of trust that Bahamian businessmen often exhibit also exerts a similar push away from capital-intensive endeavors.

[10] On the surface the scores of hotels in the Bahamas might seem a glaring exception. But, Bahamians do not own any of the major hotels. Admittedly, if we were to consider human capital, however, then the claim that capital intensive Bahamian businesses do not exist becomes difficult position to hold. The Bahamas seems overstocked with professionals; doctors, lawyers, accountants and now financial analysts abound. For instance, in a country with under 300,000 people there are 590 practicing lawyers (Virgill 2001); that's almost one lawyer for every 500 citizens.

[11] In Nassau alone there are 157 beauty salons, 152 restaurants and 39 "corner" markets (Batelco, 2000). And, 80% of the Bahamian workforce is employed in service sectors, 10-15% in industry and 5% in agriculture (World Bank, 2002 World Development Indicators).

[12] In fact, a commission of inquiry set up in 1986 to look at government involvement in the drug trade discovered that the then Prime Minister, Sir Lynden Oscar Pindling, was spending more than five times his income every year.

[13] The other five countries were Bangladesh, Indonesia, Liberia, Paraguay, and Zaire. Interestingly income per capita was higher in the Bahamas than it was in any of the other countries in this cohort.

[14] As Johnson (2000, 49) explains, "Asu(e), a means of pooling money, has a direct link to the Yorubas . . . this practice came in handy in the Bahamas where there was no bank [in the 18th and 19th centuries] from which money could be borrowed. Moreover, low-income workers who probably did not have sufficient credit to get a loan would not have been helped had there been a bank. Asu(e) obviated this. By pooling their resources, ten persons were assured of receiving a payment ten times what they contributed each week, when their hand came. The money could have been used to buy seeds, a farm animal, tools, or cloth to make garments. Asu(e) was also practiced elsewhere in the British West Indies under different names: susu in Trinidad, and partners in Jamaica."

[15] As Virgill (2001, 7) reports, "Of the 379 offshore banks in the Bahamas, only 204 or 54 percent have a physical presence in the Bahamas. However, it is usually incorrectly assumed that 'paper' centres miss out on the usual benefits of traditional banking centres such as increased employment opportunities and growth in the financial services supporting infrastructure such as telecommunications and transportation."

[16] Money laundering refers to the methods used by criminals to make the profits from their illicit activities appear legitimate. As the OECD describes, "The goal of a large number of criminal acts is to generate a profit for the individual or group that carries out the act. Money laundering is the processing of these criminal proceeds to disguise their illegal origin. This process is of critical importance, as it enables the criminal to enjoy these profits without jeopardising their source. Illegal arms sales, smuggling, and the activities of organised crime, including for example drug trafficking and prostitution rings, can generate huge sums. Embezzlement, insider trading, bribery and computer fraud schemes can also produce large profits and create the incentive to 'legitimize' the ill-gotten gains through money laundering."

[17] The Bahamas has since been removed from both lists. In December 2000, the Bahamas' government enacted a battery of laws that brought financial services in the country in line with so-called international "best practices"; it rewrote the laws that governed its offshore sector to meet OECD requirements. The new regulations, for instance, tightened the regulation of International Business Companies (IBCs), threatened financial sector practitioners (accountants, lawyers, bankers, investment advisors) who did not report suspicious transactions to the Central Bank with fines, and required that all financial institutions know their customers and the sources of their customer's income. The reaction of everyday Bahamians to the OECD's blacklisting was quite revealing. Many felt maligned (that is, unfairly put upon) and the government of the day paid a grave penalty at the polls (the FNM lost the 2002 election by a landslide) in part for seeming to cave in to international pressure.

Similar to the mood that pervaded the country in the 1980s when the Bahamas was dubbed a "nation for sale" in headline after headline in the U.S., many Bahamians responded to the blacklisting with some shame but mostly with defiance. Senator Dr. Marcus Bethel, for instance, speaking for the current government while they were in opposition, called the OECD blacklisting an "assault" (Speech in the Bahamas Senate, December 20th, 2000).

[18] This is about one fifth of the total amount deposited in Bahamian offshore accounts and only 2% of the total annual amount laundered internationally. The bulk of the money laundered by Americans, according to Walker (1999), ends up in U.S. accounts.

[19] Like the other piratical industries that have thrived in the Bahamas, offshore banking has not only benefited from the unique ability of Bahamians to identify and exploit profiteering opportunities but also encourages this peculiar orientation.

[20] James Hepple is the former Director of Planning and Information Management at the Bahamas' Ministry of Tourism.

Chapter Six
Conclusion

At its best, an interpretive act is a beam aimed at an object that was hitherto in darkness. Like a flashlight shone in a dark room used to illuminate first the dresser, then the bed, then the closet, then the door, it allows you to see what was previously obscured, it can help you to find what was previously lost. And, as with a flashlight, once the beam is redirected, once it is aimed at the bed and not the dresser, the object that was in its line of sight before retreats into darkness (or rather relative darkness). The dresser fades from view (becomes more difficult to see) when we shift our focus.

Gadamer alerts us to a similar situation when he discusses the *primacy of the question* in acts of interpretation. As Gadamer ([1960] 1989, 363) contends, "dialectic proceeds by way of question and answer or, rather, the path of all knowledge leads through the question." A person who wants to understand a text must, therefore, chase after, grope at, discover the question to which it is an answer. The question is the meaning that lies behind the text, the path into the text if you will, and discovering the question is thus the primary task of interpretation. This is as true for our understanding of assertions, or the written tradition, or works of art, as it is for our understanding of historical events. Indeed, as Gadamer (1976, 11) suggests, "no [text] is possible that cannot be understood as an answer to a question, and [texts] can only be understood in this way."

Although it is only possible to understand a text if we assume that it is an adequate answer to a question,[1] we are not required to assume that it is the only possible answer to that question. To be sure, questions "break open" the thing being questioned; they reveal that there is something indeterminate (questionable) about the thing being questioned, that there is something that is unknown that the text is attempting to make known. Rightly put questions never beg a single, set response. As Gadamer ([1960], 1989, 363) contends, "to ask a question means to bring into the open. The openness of what is in question consists in the fact that the answer is not settled." But, although a particular question can be answered (and even decisively answered) by multiple "statements" not all "statements" are possible answers to a particular question. "The openness of a question," as Gadamer (ibid.) explains, "is not boundless. It is limited by the horizon of the question. A question that lacks this horizon is, so to speak, floating." Posing a question, he continues, "implies openness but limitation." And so, the way you frame a question is extremely important because it determines the range of possible (acceptable) responses.

"How might we understand economic life in the Bahamas?", for instance, is a question that can be answered in a variety (though not an infinite number) of ways. One possible answer is that the Bahamas' protracted experience with colonialism (which was a thoroughly corrupt institutional environment), taught Bahamian entrepreneurs that success is only possible through corruption or privilege and, as a result, entrepreneurship was impeded and economic development curtailed.[2] Another possible response is that Christianity (which is the dominant religion in the Bahamas, particularly the protestant variants) so colors every aspect of social life in the Bahamas that Bahamian businesses can be readily understood as the (peculiar) attempt by Bahamian businessmen to balance their spiritual duties and their material wants. Or we might argue (as I have done here) that economic life in the Bahamas is sensibly understood as the story of two ideal typical entrepreneurs: the *enterprising slave* and the *master pirate.*

Regardless of the number of possible responses to the question ("How might we understand economic life in the Bahamas?"), however, that number is never boundless; not all "statements" made in reply to a question can be meaningfully called answers to that question. Interpretation, as Gadamer often says, is still an effort to "get it right." That the Bahamas is a communist country located just south of the equator off the coast of Ghana is a false statement and so is not a real answer to the question. Similarly, to assert that economic life appears the way it does in the Bahamas because the Bahamas is a predominantly black country is (by itself) not an adequate response to the question since the Bahamas is not the only country with a large proportion of black people and economic life differs substantially across countries that fall into that category. Remember that asking a question implies "openness" (multiple and varied answers are possible) but also "limitation" (not all possible utterances are in fact answers to the question posed).

Note also that any particular answer to a question, because it is only one of possibly many answers to that question, necessarily conceals other acceptable replies. Focusing on religion and its impact on development in the Bahamas, for instance, would (at least for that moment) blur any "image" we might have had concerning the importance of geography to the Bahamas' development efforts. Recasting the dialectic of "question" and "answer" that Gadamer employs as one of "seeing" and "saying", Wachterhauser (1999) reminds us that every story (happily) leaves out many details about the underlying phenomena it describes. As Wachterhauser (1999, 94) suggests,

> The moments of 'seeing' and 'saying,' although logically distinct, are factually inseparable from each other. This is so in the expected sense that seeing affects what we can and should say. What we see is normative for our speech and it is perfectly justifiable that speech should try to conform itself to what is there in both the perceptual and intellectual realms.

It is also perfectly justifiable that we refrain from "saying" everything that we "see" (particularly since what we "see" is often "very complex, so complex that what we see is often more than what we can say"). As Wachterhauser (ibid.) explains,

> When we understand something there is a selection (often implicit) going on not only between which aspect of the reality seen we should focus on and which we should overlook or ignore but also between which speech we should employ to bring that vision to fuller focus and which ways of speaking we should avoid lest we distort what is there. This complex process of selection is integral to the very act of interpretation itself. Interpretation occurs in the movement between intellectual intuition and linguistic discursivity.

So, it might make sense to avoid talking about the importance of the English language to development efforts in the Bahamas if that discussion would distract us or distort our understanding of the impact that corruption has had on economic life in that context. By aiming the flashlight at the bed, we might very well lose the ability to see the dresser drawers (now that they are necessarily in the shadows).[3]

This realization has enormous implications for how we ultimately use texts (which are themselves correctly understood as acts of interpretation, as answers offered in response to particular questions). Since texts necessarily conceal some of what is seen (filtering out the purported noise) in order to present a clear answer, we should be wary (particularly when the thing being seen is human activity) of any prescriptions that are said to flow from the text; they are necessarily insensitive to many of the possible side effects. This is not to say that policy recommendations are impossible to make or even that they are undesirable but only that they should be viewed with suspicion.

Indeed, policy prescriptions, in my view, are most often responses to wrongly put or slanted questions.[4] It is difficult for me to see, I must confess, how a recommendation that would eliminate or constrain dialogue or close off meaningful discussion or that would curtail economic freedoms (which amounts to the same thing) could be thought of as an answer to a rightly put question. Similarly, it is difficult for me to imagine any basket of regulations and reforms that can (honestly) be said to have followed from my or anyone else's understanding of economic life in the Bahamas. At best, I can offer an unguarded assertion that economic life is a discourse and that discourses whether they are conversations or markets should be made as free as possible. As Lavoie (1992, 450) suggests of a truly open and open-ended discursive process, "we cannot [hope to] control it; all we can do is establish the conditions in which it will flourish and then take our guidance from it."

The Bahamas' economic story is, if nothing else, an interesting tale. It is not only a story of short-lived booms followed by protracted busts but it is also a tale of color, vibrant color, where discussions of economic success force us to mention almost fanciful figures like Blackbeard and Calico Jack and where accounts of economic woe (like the collapse of the cotton market) are punctuated by descriptions of the clamor of Sunday markets or the unique practice of self-hire. I have told the economic story of the Bahamas as a tale with two leading characters. The first one, the *master pirate* was meant to be neither the villain nor the hero of this plot. Although the narrow radiuses of trust that are often associated with his activities and the high time preference that affects his investment decisions are certainly an impediment to long term economic development, his eagerness to exploit even dubious profit opportunities, his cunning, his guile, is as responsible for what economic success this nation has enjoyed as any other factor. Indeed, all of the Bahamas' successful industries (including off-shore banking and tourism) have relied on this character (and have sustained and promoted him for that matter).

The second character, the *enterprising slave,* is a similarly intriguing figure. Much of her attitudes and temperament can be traced back to the African continent (where most of the Bahamas' population descends from). Her *spirit of enterprise,* her willingness to work hard even in the face of extreme obstacles explains how she was able to survive such a damnable system like slavery and, if we are to be frank, is (at least in part) what made her so attractive to slavers in the first place. That she remains a dominant figure in even contemporary Bahamian economic narratives only makes her a more interesting character.

As I have argued, it is the interplay of these two colorful characters, the *fractured consciousnesses* that result when Bahamian entrepreneurs try to integrate the lessons they learn from these two figures, the schizophrenia that Craton and Saunders (1992, 104) discussed, that makes their story one that is worth (re)telling. Admittedly, I have focused (sometimes clumsily even) on only a fraction of what is the entire Bahamian economic story (much of interest may lie un-illuminated by the narrow beam I cast, much of the room still remains in darkness). But, this tale, I believe, was an important one to tell.

E bob en my story done en', I swear I'll never tell a lie like dat again. [5]

Notes

[1] Gadamer has called this the "fore-conception of completeness." As Gadamer ([1960], 1989, 294) contends, "only what constitutes a unity of meaning is intelligible. So when we read a text we always assume its completeness, and only when this assumption proves mistaken – i.e., the text is not intelligible – do we begin to suspect the text."

[2] Indeed, I explored precisely this point in *All We've Learnt: Colonial Teachings and Caribbean Underdevlopment* (2002) where I asserted that because of colonialism "many of the stories told in West Indian [including Bahamian] societies are pessimistic tales about the possibility of economic success and optimistic fables about the potential of government intervention. The region's cultural texts associate prosperity with bribes, kickbacks, political connections or racial privilege. And, the region's history is littered with one government intervention into the economy after another; subsidies, tariff protections, bailouts, government initiation of new enterprises, favoring of foreign enterprises and acquisition of failing ones are exceedingly common. These *cultures of intervention, privilege and corruption* have distorted entrepreneurial creativity and diminished entrepreneurial efforts by reducing the perceived payoffs to entrepreneurship. Consequently, economic development has been impeded."

[3] Madison makes an analogous point when he describes the "deceitfulness" of metaphors. As he suggests, "to see something as something else (my loved one as a rose, man as a wolf) requires at the same time the realization that one thing is not the other thing (if this is not realized, the metaphor ceases to be a metaphor). To say that something is like something else is to say that it both is and is not that other thing" (Madison 1982,211 cited in Madison 1988, 147). By directing us towards a particular

way of seeing some thing, a metaphor admittedly aims us away from other (likely legitimate) ways of seeing that thing (my loved one as a viper, man as an angel).

[4] As Gadamer ([1960], 1989, 362-363) asserts, "a question can be asked rightly or wrongly, according as [to whether] it reaches into the sphere of the truly open or fails to do so. We say that a question has been put wrongly when it does not reach the state of openness but precludes reaching it by retaining false presuppositions. It pretends to an openness and susceptibility to decision that it does not have. But if what is in question is not foregrounded, or not correctly foregrounded, from those presuppositions that are really held, then it is not brought into the open and nothing can be decided." Economic policy recommendations, for instance, are often asked for in a way that assumes that government needs to be proactive (read interventionist) and so prescriptions (based on this kind of questioning) can not (honestly) be said to follow from open questions. As Gadamer (ibid.) continues, "This is shown clearly in the case of the slanted question that we are so familiar with in everyday life. There can be no [real] answer to a slanted question because it leads us only apparently, and not really, through the open state of indeterminacy in which a decision is made. We call it slanted rather than wrongly put because there is a question behind it – i.e., there is an openness intended, but it does not lie in the direction in which the slanted question is pointing."

[5] Traditional Bahamian refrain, usually recited after recounting a story or telling a folktale in the Bahamas.

Bibliography

Albury, Paul 1975. *The Story of the Bahamas.* London: The Macmillan Education Ltd.

Arrow, Kenneth J. 2000. 'Observations on social capital' in *Social Capital: A Multifaceted Perspective* ed. P. Dasgupta and I. Serageldin (Washington, DC: World Bank.).

Baker, Christopher P. 1998. *Bahamas, Turks & Caicos.* Oakland: Lonely Planet Publications.

Baumol, William J. 1990. 'Entrepreneurship: Productive, Unproductive, and Destructive.' *Accounting, Organizations and Society* 12: 579-604.

Beckles, Hilary 1990. *A History of Barbados: From Amerindian settlement to nation-state.* Cambridge, UK: Cambridge University Press.

Beckles, Hilary and Verne Shepherd 1990. *Caribbean Freedom: Society and Economy From Emancipation to the Present.* Kingston, Jamaica: Ian Randle Publishers.

Beckles, Hilary and Verne Shepherd 1991. *Caribbean Slave Society and Economy.* New York, NY: The New York Press.

Berger, Peter 1994. 'On Economic Culture' in *The Cultural Context of Economics and Politics* ed. T.W. Boxx and G.M. Quinlivan (Lanham: University Press of America, Inc.).

Bethel, Felix 1989. 'Tourism, Public Policy, and National Development' in *Caribbean Modern Bahamian Society* ed. D.W. Collinwood and S. Dodge (Parkersburg, IA: Caribbean Books).

Bird-David, Nurit 1992a "Beyond 'The Affluent Society': A Culturalist Reformation," and Discussion. *Current Anthropology* 33: 25-34.

Bird-David, Nurit 1992b "Beyond 'The Hunting and Gathering Mode of Subsistence': Culture-Sensitive Observations on the Nayaka and Other Modern Hunter-Gatherers." *Man* 27: 19-44.

Black, Clinton V. 1989. *Pirates of the West Indies.* Cambridge: Cambridge University Press.

Boettke, Peter J. 1994. *The Elgar Companion to Austrian Economics.* Northampton, MA: Edward Elgar Publishing, Inc.

Boettke, Peter J. 1995a. 'Individuals and Institutions' in *Individuals, Institutions, Interpretations* ed. D.L. Prychitko (Burlington: Ashgate Publishing Company).

Boettke, Peter J. 1995b. 'Interpretive Reasoning and the Study of Social Life' in *Individuals, Institutions, Interpretations* ed. D.L. Prychitko (Burlington: Ashgate Publishing Company).

Boettke, Peter J. 1998. "Rational Choice and Human Agency in Economics and Sociology" in *Merits and Limits of Markets* ed. H. Giersch, Berlin: Springer-Verlag.

Boettke, Peter J. 2001. 'Why culture matters: economics, politics, and the imprint of history.' in *Calculation and Coordination* ed. Peter Boettke (New York: Routledge).

Boettke, Peter J. and Virgil H. Storr 2002. 'Post Classical Political Economy: Polity, Society and Economy in Weber, Mises and Hayek.' *American Journal of Economics and Sociology*, 61 no. 1.

Butkevich, Bridget and Virgil H. Storr, 2001. 'Cultural Characters: How Entrepreneurs Respond in Hostile Climates.' *Working Paper.*

Cash, Philip, Shirley Gordon and Gail Saunders. 1991. *Sources of Bahamian History.* London: The Macmillan Press Ltd.

Chamlee-Wright, Emily 1997. *The Cultural Foundations of Economic Development: Urban Female Entrepreneurship in Ghana.* New York, NY: Routledge.

Collinwood, Dean W. 1989a. 'The Bahamas in Social Transition' in *Caribbean Modern Bahamian Society* ed. D.W. Collinwood and S. Dodge (Parkersburg, IA: Caribbean Books).

Collinwood, Dean W. 1989b. 'Themes in Modern Bahamian Literature' in *Caribbean Modern Bahamian Society* ed. D.W. Collinwood and S. Dodge (Parkersburg, IA: Caribbean Books).

Collinwood, Dean W. and Steve Dodge 1989. *Modern Bahamian Society*. Parkersburg, IA: Caribbean Books.

Coppin, Clayton A. and Jack High 1999. *The Politics of Purity: Harvey Washington Wiley and the Origins of Federal Food Policy*. Ann Arbor, MI: The University of Michigan Press.

Cordingly, David 1995. *Under the Black Flag: The Romance and the Reality of Life Among the Pirates*. Orlando: Harcourt Brace & Company.

Craton, Michael [1962] 1986. *A History of the Bahamas*. Waterloo, Canada: San Salvador Press.

Craton, Michael and Gail Saunders 1992. *Islanders in the Stream: A History of the Bahamian People (Volume One: From Aboriginal Times to the End of Slavery)*. Athens, GA: The University of Georgia Press.

Craton, Michael and Gail Saunders 1998. *Islanders in the Stream: A History of the Bahamian People (Volume Two: From the Ending of Slavery to the Twenty-First Century)*. Athens, GA: The University of Georgia Press.

Defoe, Daniel [1724] 1972. *A General History of the Pyrates*. Mineola, NY: Dover Publications, Inc.

Dewey, John [1925] 1929. *Experience and Nature*. Chicago, IL: Open Court.

Dewey, John 1929 . The *Quest for Certainty: A Study of the Relation of Knowledge and Action*. New York: Minton, Balch & Co.

Dewey, John [1938] 1991. *Logic: The Theory Of Inquiry*. Volume 12 (1938) of The Later Works, 1925-1953. Carbondale, IL: Southern Illinois University Press.

Dewey, John 1973. *The Philosophy of John Dewey (Two Volumes in One): 1 The Structure of Experience, 2 The Lived Experience*. Chicago, IL: The University of Chicago Press.

Du Bois, W.E.B. [1903] 1969. *The Souls of Black Folks*. New York, NY: Signet Classic.

Dunn, Richard S. 1972. *Sugar and Slaves: The Rise of the Planter Class in the English West Indies, 1624-1713*. New York, NY: W. W. Norton & Company.

Easterly, William 2001. *The Elusive Quest for Growth: Economists' Adventures and Misadventures in the Tropics*. Cambridge: The MIT Press.

Ebeling, Richard M. 1990. "What is a price? Explaination and understanding (with apologies to Paul Ricoeur" in *Economics and Hermeneutics* ed. D. Lavoie (London, UK: Routledge).

Eneas, Wm. J. Godfrey 1998. *Agriculture in the Bahamas: Historical Development 1492-1992*. Nassau: Media Publishing.

Ferguson, Arlene Nash 2000. *I Come To Get Me! An inside look at the Junkanoo Festival.* Nassau: Doongalik Studios.

Francis, Carlene 1987. 'Offshore Banking in The Bahamas' in *Business Practice in the Bahamas: A Book of Readings* ed. T. Sharma (Nassau, Bahamas: College of the Bahamas).

Fukuyama, Francis 1995. *Trust: The Social Virtues and the Creation of Prosperity.* New York, NY: Free Press Paperbacks.

Gadamer, Hans-Georg 1976. *Philosophical Hermeneutics.* Berkeley, CA: University of Califonia Press.

Gadamer, Hans-Georg 1986. *The Relevance of The Beautiful And Other Essays.* New York, NY: Cambridge University Press.

Gadamer, Hans-Georg [1960] 1989. *Truth and Method.* New York: Crossroad.

Geertz, Clifford 1963. *Peddlers and Princes: Social Development and Economic Growth in Two Indonesian Towns.* Princeton, NJ: Princeton University Press.

Geertz, Clifford 2000. *Available Light: Anthropological Reflections on Philosophical Topics.* Princeton, NJ: Princeton University Press.

Gerassi-Navarro, Nina 1993. *An Evening in Guanima: A Treasury of Folktales from The Bahamas.* Nassau, N.P: Guanima Press.

Glinton, Patricia 1999. *Pirate Novels: Fictions of Nation Building in Spanish America.* Durham: Duke University Press.

Glinton-Meicholas, Patricia 1994. *How to be a true-true Bahamian: a hilarious look at life in the Bahamas.* Nassau, N.P: Guanima Press.

Glinton-Meicholas, Patricia 1995. *More Talkin' Bahamian..* Nassau, N.P: Guanima Press.

Glinton-Meicholas, Patricia 1998. *The 99¢ Breakfast*. Nassau, N.P: Guanima Press.

Glinton-Meicholas, Patricia 2001a. *Robin's Song*. Nassau, N.P: Guanima Press.

Glinton-Meicholas, Patricia 2001b. *No Vacancy in Paradise*. Nassau, N.P: Guanima Press.
Gosse, Philip 1995. *The History of Piracy*. Glorieta, NM: The Rio Grande Press, Inc..

Granovetter, Mark 1985. 'Economic Action and Social Structure: The Problem of Embeddedness.' *American Journal of Sociology* 91: 481-510.

Granovetter, Mark 1992. 'Economic Institutions as Social Constructions: A Framework for Analysis.' *Acta Sociologica* 35: 3-11.

Gudeman, Stephen 1986. *Economics as Culture: Models and Metaphors of Livelihood*. London: Routledge.

Hall, N. A. T. 1991. 'Slave Use of Their 'Free' Time in the Danish Virgin Islands in the later Eighteenth and Early Nineteenth Century' in *Caribbean Slave Society and Economy* ed. H. Beckles and V. Shepherd (New York, NY: The New York Press).

Hammersley, Martyn and Paul Atkinson 1995. *Ethnography: Principles in Practice*. New York, NY: Routledge.

Harrison, Lawrence E. 1985. *Underdevelopment is a State of Mind: The Latin American Case*. New York, NY: Madison Books.

Harrison, Lawrence E. 1992. *Who Prospers: How Cultural Values Shape Economic and Political Success*. New York, NY: Basic Books.

Harrison, Lawrence E. and Samuel P. Huntington 2000. *Culture Matters: How Values Shape Human Progress*. New York, NY: Basic Books.

Hayek, F. A. 1948. *Individualism and Economic Order*. Chicago, IL: The University of Chicago Press.

Hayek, Friedrich A. 1960. *The Constitution of Liberty*. Chicago, IL: The University of Chicago Press.

Higgins, J. Kevin 1994. *The Bahamian Economy: An Analysis*. Nassau, Bahamas: The Counsellors Ltd.

High, Jack 1990. *Maximizing, Action, and Market Adjustment: An Inquiry into the Theory of Economic Disequilibrium.* Muchen, Hamden: Philosophia.

Hill, Polly 1986. *Development Economics on Trial: The Anthropological Case for a Prosecution.* New York, NY: Cambridge University Press.

Jenkins, Olga Culmer 2000. *Bahamian Memories: Island Voices of the Twentieth Century.* Gainesville, FL: University Press of Florida.

Johnson, Doris L. 1972. *The Quiet Revolution in the Bahamas.* Nassau, NP: The Family Island Press Limited.

Johnson, Howard 1996. *The Bahamas from Slavery to Servitude: 1783-1933.* Gainesville, FL: University Press of Florida.

Johnson, Whittington B. 2000. *Race Relations in the Bahamas: 1784-1834.* Fayetteville: The University of Arkansas Press.

Klamer, Arjo 1990. "Towards the native's point of view: the difficulty of changing the conversation" in *Economics and Hermeneutics* ed. D. Lavoie (London, UK: Routledge).

Klein, Herbert S. 1986. *African Slavery in Latin America and the Caribbean.* New York, NY: Oxford University Press.

Kincaid, Jamaica 1988. *A Small Place.* New York, NY: Plume.

Kirzner, Israel M. 1973. *Competition & Entrepreneurship.* Chicago, IL: The University of Chicago Press.

Kirzner, Israel M. 1979. *Perception, Opportunity, and Profit: Studies in the Theory of Entrepreneurship.* Chicago, IL: The University of Chicago Press.

Kirzner, Israel M. 1994. 'Entrepreneurship.' in *The Elgar Companion to Austrian Economics* ed. Peter Boettke (Northampton, MA: Edward Elgar Publishing, Inc).

Kirzner, Israel M. 1999. 'Creativity and/or Alertness: A Reconsideration of the Shumpertarian Entrepreneur.' *The Review of Austrian Economics* 11: 5-17.

Knight, Franklin W. 1990. *The Caribbean: The Genesis of a Fragmented Nationalism.* New York, NY: Oxford University Press.

Kulii, Elon A. and Beverly Threatt Kulii 2001. 'Brer Rabbit.' in *The Concise Oxford Companion to African American Literature* ed. W. L. Andrews, F. S. Foster and T. Harris (New York: Oxford University Press).

Lachmann, Ludwig M. 1971. *The Legacy of Max Weber.* Berkeley: Glendessary Press.

Lachmann, Ludwig M. 1977. *Capital, Expectations, and the Market Process: Essays on the Theory of the Market Economy.* Kansas City, Kansas: Sheed Andrews and McMeel, Inc.

Lachmann, Ludwig M. 1990. "Austrian economics: a hermeneutic approach" in *Economics and Hermeneutics* ed. D. Lavoie (London, UK: Routledge).

Lachmann, Ludwig M. 1994. *Expectations and the Meaning of Institutions: Essays in Economics by Ludwig Lachmann.* London: Routledge.

Lalta, Stanley and Marie Freckleton 1993. *Caribbean Economic Development: The First Generation.* Kingston, Jamaica: Ian Randle Publishers.

Lamming, George 1983. *In the Castle of My Skin.* Ann Arbor, MI: The University of Michigan Press.

Lane, Kris E. 1998. *Blood & Silver: A History of Piracy in the Caribbean and Central America.* Oxford: Signal Books Ltd.

Lavoie, Don 1985. *National Economic Planning: What is Left?* Cambridge, Mass.: Ballinger.

Lavoie, Don 1987. 'The Accounting of Interpretations and the Interpretation of Accounts: The Communicative Function of 'The Language of Business."' *Accounting, Organizations and Society* 12: 579-604.

Lavoie, Don 1990. *Economics and Hermeneutics.* London, UK: Routledge.

Lavoie, Don 1990b. 'Hermeneutics, Subjectivity, and the Lester/Machlup Debate: Toward a More Anthropological Approach to Empirical Economics' in *Economics as Discourse* ed. W. Samuels (Boston: Kluwer Academic Publishing).

Lavoie, Don 1990c. 'Understanding Differently: Hermeneutics and the Spontaneous Order of Communicative Processes.' *History of Political Economy.* Annual Supplement to 22: 359-377.

Lavoie, Don 1991. 'The Discovery and Interpretation of Profit Opportunities: Culture and the Kirznerian Entrepreneur' in *The Culture of Entrepreneurship* ed. B. Berger (San Francisco: CA: ICS Press).

Lavoie, Don 1994. 'Cultural Studies and the Conditions for Entrepreneurship' in *The Cultural Context of Economics and Politics* ed. T.W. Boxx and G.M. Quinlivan (Lanham: University Press of America, Inc.).

Lavoie, Don 1995a. 'The market as a procedure for the discovery and conveyance of inarticulate knowledge' in *Individuals, Institutions, Interpretations* ed. D.L. Prychitko (Burlington: Ashgate Publishing Company).

Lavoie, Don and Emily Chamlee-Wright 2001. *Culture And Enterprise: The Development, Representation, and Morality of Business* (New York, NY: Routledge).

Lavoie, Don and Virgil Storr 2001. 'As a Consequence of Meaning: Rethinking the Relationship between Thymology and Praxeology,' *Working Paper*.

Levitt, Kari and Lloyd Best 1993. 'Character of the Caribbean Economy' in *Caribbean Freedom: Economy and Society from Emancipation to the Present* ed. H. Beckles and V. Shepherd (Kingston, Jamaica: Ian Randle Publishers).

Lewis, Matthew [1834] 1999. *Journal of a West India Proprietor*. Oxford, UK: Oxford University Press.

Leys, Colin 1996. *The Rise & Fall of Development Theory*. Bloomington, IN: Indiana University Press.

Lipset, Seymour Martin 1990. *Continental Divide: The Values and Institutions of the United States and Canada*. New York, NY: Routledge.

Madison, G.B. 1988. *The Hermeneutic of Postmodernity: Figures and Themes*. Bloomington: Indiana University Press.

Madison, G.B. 1990. "Getting beyond objectivism: the philosophical hermeneutics of Gadamer and Ricoeur" in *Economics and Hermeneutics* ed. D. Lavoie (London, UK: Routledge).

Madison, G.B. 1995a. 'How individualistic is methodological individualism' in *Individuals, Institutions, Interpretations* ed. D.L. Prychitko (Burlington: Ashgate Publishing Company).

Marine Research Society 1837. *The Pirates Own Book: Authentic Narratives of the Most Celebrated Sea Robbers*. New York: Dover Publications.

McCloskey, Deirdre 2000a. *How to Be Human: Though an Economist*. Ann Arbor, MI: The University of Michigan Press.

McCloskey, Deirdre 2000b. *Economical Writing*. Prospect Heights, IL: Waveland Press, Inc.

McCloskey, Donald N. 1985. *The Rhetoric of Economics*. Madison, WI: The University of Wisconsin Press.

McCloskey, Donald N. 1990a. *If You're So Smart: The Narrative of Economic Expertise*. Chicago, IL: The University of Chicago Press.

McCloskey, Donald N. 1990b. 'Storytelling in economics' in *Economics and Hermeneutics* ed. D. Lavoie (London, UK: Routledge).

McFarlane, Andrian Anthony 1998. 'The Epistemological Significance of 'I-an-I' as a Response to Quashie and Anancyism in Jamaican Culture' in *Chanting Down Babylon* ed. N.S. Murrell, W.D. Spencer and A. A. McFarlane (Philadelphia, PA: Temple University Press).

Mintz, Sidney W. 1993. 'The Origins of Reconstituted Peasantries' in *Caribbean Freedom: Economy and Society from Emancipation to the Present* ed. H. Beckles and V. Shepherd (Kingston, Jamaica: Ian Randle Publishers).

Mintz, Sidney W. and Douglas Hall 1970. 'The Origins of the Jamaican Internal Marketing System' in *Papers in Caribbean Anthropology* ed. S. Mintz (New Haven, CT: Human Relations Area Files Press).

Mises, Ludwig von [1934]1963. *Human Action: A Treatise on Economics*. Third Revised Edition. San Francisco, CA: Fox & Wilkes.

North, Douglass C. 1990. *Institutions, Institutional Change and Economic Performance*. New York, NY: Cambridge University Press.

North, Douglass C. 1995. 'The New Institutional Economics and Third World Development' in *The New Institutional Economics and Third World Development* ed. J. Harriss, J. Hunter and C. Lewis (New York, NY: Routledge).

Powles, L. D. [1888] 1996. *The Land of the Pink Pearl: Recollections of Life in the Bahamas*. Nassau: Media Publishing.

Prychitko, David L. 1995. *Individuals, Institutions, Interpretations: Hermeneutics Applied to Economics.* Burlington: Ashgate Publishing Company.

Ramsaran, Ramesh 1989. 'The Bahamas: An Assessment of Post-Independence Economic Experience' in *Caribbean Modern Bahamian Society* ed. D.W. Collinwood and S. Dodge (Parkersburg, IA: Caribbean Books).

Riley, Sandra 1983. *Homeward Bound: A History of the Bahama Islands to 1850.* Miami: Island Research.

Rogozinski, Jan 1992. *A Brief History of the Caribbean: From The Arawak and The Carib To The Present.* New York, NY: Meridian.

Saunders, Gail 1985. *Slavery in The Bahamas: 1648-1838.* Nassau, Bahamas: The Nassau Guardian.

Saunders, Gail 1990. *Bahamian Society After Emancipation.* Kingston, Jamaica: Ian Randle Publishers Limited.

Schutz, Alfred [1932] 1967. *The Phenomenology of the Social World.* Evanston: Northwestern University Press

Schumpeter, Joseph A. [1934] 1983. *The Theory of Economic Development.* New Brunswick, NJ: Transaction Publishers.

Sowell, Thomas 1985. *Marxism: Philosophy and Economics.* New York: Quill.

Sherlock, Philip and Hazel Bennett 1998. *The Story of the Jamaican People* (Kingston, Jamaica: Ian Randle Publishers).

St. Cyr, Eric 1993. 'The Theory of Caribbean-Type Economy' in *Caribbean Economic Development* ed. S.Lalta and M. Freckleton (Kingston, Jamaica: Ian Randle Publishers).

Strachan, Ian Gregory 1995. *Paradise and Plantation: The Economy of Caribbean Discourse.* Unpublished Dissertation.

Storr, Virgil 1996. 'Caribbean Economic Integration and Public Choice.' *Working Paper.*

Storr, Virgil 2000a. 'Expulsis Piratis?: The Enduring Culture of Bahamian Entrepreneurs.' *Working Paper.*

Storr, Virgil 2000b. 'Sankofa: Slavery and the Bahamas' Relative Prosperity.' *Working Paper.*

Storr, Virgil 2002. 'All We've Learnt: Colonial Teachings and Caribbean Underdevelopment.' *Journal des Economistes et des Etudes Humaines,* 12 (4).

Storr, Virgil and Nicola Virgill 1999. 'Off-shore Banking.' *Working Paper.*

Swedberg, Richard 1998. *Max Weber and the Idea of Economic Sociology.* Princeton: Princeton University Press.

Thompson, Alvin O. 1997. *The Haunting Past: Politics, Economics and Race in Caribbean Life.* Armonk, NY: M.E. Sharpe.

Thompson, Anthony A. 1979. *An Economic History of the Bahamas.* Nassau: Commonwealth Publications Limited.

Throsby, David 2001. *Economics and Culture.* Cambridge, UK: Cambridge University Press.

Tomich, Dale W. 1991. 'The Other Face of Slave Labor: Provision Grounds and Internal Marketing in Martinique' in *Caribbean Slave Society and Economy* ed. H. Beckles and V. Shepherd (New York, NY: The New York Press).

Trompenaars, Fons and Charles Hampden-Turner 1998. *Riding the Waves of Culture: Understanding Cultural Diversity in Global Business.* New York, NY: McGraw-Hill.

Turner, Telcine 1988. *Once Below a Time: Bahamian Stories.* London, UK: McMillan Education Ltd.

Turner, Telcine 1988b. *Climbing Clouds: Stories and Poems from the Bahamas.* London, UK: McMillan Education Ltd.

van der Valk, H. M. H. A. 1979. *Economics applied to The Bahamas.* Nassau: The Central Bank of the Bahamas.

Virgill, Nicola 2001. 'Whither OffShore Banking? An Institutional Analysis of Offshore Banking in the Bahamas.' *Unpublished Master's Thesis.*

Wachterhauser, Brice R. 1994. *Hermeneutics and Truth.* Evanston, IL: Northwestern University Press.

Wachterhauser, Brice R. 1999. *Beyond Being: Gadamer's Post-Platonic Hermeneutical Ontology*. Evanston, IL: Northwestern University Press.

Walvin, James. 1992. *Black Ivory: A History of British Slavery*. London, UK: Fontana Press.

Weber, Max 1947. *The Theory of Social and Economic Organization*. New York, NY: The Free Press.

Weber, Max [1921] 1978. *Economy and Society: An Outline of Interpretive Sociology*, two volumes. Berkeley: University of California Press.

Weber, Max. [1930] 1992. *The Protestant Ethic and the Spirit of Capitalism*. London, UK: Routledge.

Weber, Max [1949] 1997. *Methodology of the Social Sciences*. Glencoe, Ill.: Free Press.

Weber, Max 1999. *Essays in Economic Sociology*. Princeton, NJ: Princeton University Press.

Williams, Eric. 1970. *From Columbus to Castro: The History of the Caribbean*. New York, NY: Vintage Books.

Wilk, Richard R. 1996. *Economies & Cultures: Foundations of Economic Anthropology*. Boulder, CO: Westview Press.

Wood, Vivian Nina Michelle 1995. *Rushin' Hard and Runnin' Hot: Experiencing The Music of the Junkanoo Parade in Nassau, Bahamas*. Unpublished Dissertation.

Index

E

F

G

H

I

J

K

L

M

N

O

P

R

S

T

V

W